Ten Steps on Freedom Road

Ten Steps on Freedom Road

Why the Commandments are Good News

JOHN BADERTSCHER

RESOURCE *Publications* · Eugene, Oregon

TEN STEPS ON FREEDOM ROAD
Why the Commandments are Good News

Resource Publications
An Imprint of Wipf and Stock Publishers
199 W. 8th Ave., Suite 3
Eugene, OR 97401

www.wipfandstock.com

PAPERBACK ISBN: 978–1-5326–9395-3
HARDCOVER ISBN: 978–1-5326–9396-0
EBOOK ISBN: 978–1-5326–9397-7

Manufactured in the U.S.A.   04/18/19

To the people of Bristol Methodist Church,
St. Mark's Lutheran Church,
Knox United Church,
and Clandeboye United Church,
who allowed me to teach and to learn from their children.

Contents

Preface

I WRITE THIS, NOT with the hope of publication and many readers, but because my time and energy are growing short, and there are things I want my children, grandchildren and surviving friends to hear from me. These words are feeble attempts to express what I have come to see as some of the most important things I have to share with those I love. This is what the Methodists of my childhood would have called "testimony."

At its worst, testimony becomes an over-dramatic, self-centered display of self-righteousness or misplaced and unjustified certainty. Should this testimony fall into one of those traps, I beg the reader's forgiveness. All too often, testimony becomes the repetition of old formulae without sufficient critical awareness and personal engagement. When my words seem to fail in this way, I ask the reader to take it as a sign of my limited imagination and a lack of power to engage in genuine wrestling with voices from the past and visions from the future. I further beg the reader to engage with these voices herself/himself, to do me the honor of carrying on the conversation when I have failed to do so.

At its best, my testimony is a way of sharing what it means to me to "love God with all your heart, and soul, and mind, and strength; and love your neighbor as yourself." I know that words alone cannot express love; but I believe that, for human beings, love demands verbal expression as well as actions. It is up to others to judge whether my actions are adequate expressions of love. These words are a love letter to life.

I have been inspired by these words from the journals of Arvo Pärt, as they appeared in *The Christian Century*, December 19, 2018:

> *Living according to God's commandments is literally a creative activity. I am not telling you this as though I myself might have accomplished something here. But I am completely persuaded that every step is then a discovery, through tears and sweat, of course: a chain of losses and findings, of self-transcendence, of falling and getting up again.*

1

The Shape of Freedom

FOR MANY PEOPLE, RELIGION is understood to consist of two parts: beliefs and rules. Beliefs can be seen as arbitrary rules for thinking and imagining, easily dismissed as lacking empirical evidence and therefore as matters of private, individual judgment. The related rules then appear as arbitrary limitations on human actions. Once beliefs and rules are so understood, religion can be classified as acceptable, tolerable in a free society as a matter of private and unaccountable judgment. Religion, then, is seen as a non-rational set of beliefs connected to a non-rational set of rules that one might, for whatever reason, choose to live by. This is not my understanding of a life of faith.

Freedom, for many people, is also seen as something pertaining to individuals. When we say that we live in a free country, we pass by the older sense that our political community is free because it is self-governing, making its own laws. Rather, we mean that our government is constrained to place the fewest possible restrictions on what we do, say, and think. Freedom, understood this way, is at its greatest when each individual can choose without restraint what to do, say, and think. This freedom is limited only by the presence of other free persons within the sphere of one's life. Within this way of understanding freedom, it is hard to imagine why anyone would accept the rules, including the mental rules called beliefs or creeds, which any religious or other tradition or community would impose upon one's freedom. We might be "spiritual," however that is understood; but to be religious, in this sense, is to surrender one's freedom. This is not my understanding of freedom.

The set of laws I intend to explore here are usually called the Ten Commandments or, in a Jewish context, the Ten Words. In what follows, I will be giving testimony to how I have come to acknowledge the Ten Commandments as offering us a better, truer path of freedom. In the course of this testimony, I will be challenging the way many people understand freedom and faith. My challenge will also have implications for the way religion is best to be understood. If this were a more philosophical writing, I might begin by redefining these basic terms. Instead, I simply warn the reader that the challenge is present. I will try to present a different and better understanding of freedom as we go. When we have finished our explorations, we can return to these matters to see whether more adequate understandings of faith and freedom are available.

These deeper ways of understanding freedom and faith are by no means original with me. I have been blessed by great teachers, some of them academic. With two exceptions, I choose not to name them here. I would rather that the conversation simply be between the reader and me. The two teachers I must acknowledge here are Walter Harrelson and Krister Stendahl. Harrelson, a man whom I never met, was a twentieth century Christian scholar of what is usually called the Old Testament. He published several books on the Ten Commandments and devoted himself to Jewish-Christian dialogue. Readers who want a scholarly treatment of the themes we will be exploring should consult his writings, still in print. His way of connecting the Ten Commandments to freedom has been formative for me. I thank Krister Stendahl, New Testament scholar and Bishop of the Church of Sweden, for a six-week course in the summer of 1959 which opened my eyes to a new reading of Paul's letter to the Romans. Whatever wisdom there is in my treatment of that text, and in my understanding of the relation between Jesus' teachings and the Ten Commandments, I owe to him.

Now we begin by showing how each of the Ten Commandments offers genuine freedom to those who would take them seriously, and how each of them gives us a path we can walk joyfully.

2

Law and Story

IT IS POSSIBLE TO imagine the Ten Commandments floating down from the sky, as if God were saying: "This is the way it has to be. These are the conditions under which you must live unless you want me to get really angry with you." People whose parents or caregivers were strict or impatient or just plain mean might imagine the relationship between God and humans that way. But that is not the way the law appears in the Bible. In fact, no human community I know of has arrived at their laws that way. Laws always emerge as part of a story. People live together, make mistakes, hurt each other and, at their best, try to learn from what goes wrong. A law is always set in a story, although law-makers and judges are not always aware of the stories that are shaping their decisions. Strict, impatient, or mean parents and caregivers have their own stories, of which they may or may not be conscious. Sometimes when children are grown, they come to a point where they suddenly can say to themselves: "Aha! So that is why Mom or Dad was that way." Embedded in a story, every law thus reflects experiences in which people have come to see some patterns of action as wrong and hurtful. No community has ever passed a law against something that no one was doing. So laws do not tell us: "In our community no one does this." Rather, they tell us that such things have been done, and are done often enough that we have come to see how wrong and hurtful they are. Laws are both evidence of human brokenness and visions of human fulfillment. This evidence is remembered and these visions are carried in stories.

So the Ten Commandments cannot be understood except as part of a story. They do not appear at the beginning of the story, and their meaning develops continually throughout the story. Jews and Christians, and in a way Muslims too, share this story. Of course there are important differences in the way the story is told and interpreted, not just between Jews and Christians, but within each group. I am writing as a Christian of a particular kind, and I know my "take" on the commandments will be different, sometimes very different, from that of others, even other Christians. As I try to interpret the Commandments in a way that is faithful to the story we share, I know my understanding is limited and fallible, and that others will see them differently. That does not make my testimony less serious.

As a Christian, I see the story leading to Jesus of Nazareth: his life, his teachings, his death and his resurrection. For Christians, the meaning of the Commandments is understood as leading toward, through and beyond Jesus. The story comes to us through the community (the church) Jesus called together, and which his Spirit continues to lead, however poorly we may follow. We have our own mistakes, wrongs and hurts which we have inflicted on ourselves and others; and we have our own story-tellers, especially in the gospels and letters of the New Testament. My understanding of the Commandments is shaped by that experience and tradition. The New Testament sometimes portrays Jesus as a lawgiver. Some Christians have come to see the laws of the New Testament as different from and superior to those of the scriptures we share with Jews. Of course, the Christian version of the story in which the Commandments are located is different from the Jewish version; but I am more impressed by how much is shared. I have come to see that the New Testament simply cannot be sensibly understood apart from the Original ("Old") Testament, and that the truth of the New Testament validates and, I would claim, clarifies the truth of the Original Testament. I will have something to say about the teachings of Jesus on the commandments later. But first I want us to see the Ten Commandments in the context of the story Jews and Christians (and, in their own way, Muslims) share.

3

The Big Picture

IF YOU WANT TO know the whole story, you have to read the Bible. It is a great collection of writings, written originally in Hebrew, Aramaic and Greek and available in a bewildering variety of translations, each of which reflects the insights, culture and limitations of the translators. The Bible is a weird and wonderful collection. It does not simply tell a story, but is also made up of smaller stories, poetry and other kinds of writing. The whole story emerges from the collection only with the help of the reader's imagination. I do not say these things to discourage you from reading the Bible, for that is something I very much hope you will (continue?) to do; but to approach the Bible without an awareness of its character, its weirdness if you please, will lead the reader to give up in confusion or despair, or to turn to some supposed authority for oversimplified help that is finally disrespectful of the book itself. So this is a "heads up."

One of the most important figures in the story is a man named Jacob. He is a rascal. Having cheated his brother, Jacob leaves home to seek his fortune and avoid the consequences of his misdeeds. Much later he returns home, family and fortune in tow. However, he is still afraid of his brother and the army his brother has come to lead. So when Jacob gets to the border of his brother's turf, he sends his family across but waits on the far side with his demons. During a restless night, he is confronted by a mysterious presence with whom he wrestles. At dawn the match ends in a draw, with Jacob demanding from the stranger a blessing. The stranger vanishes, after "blessing" Jacob with a dislocated hip and a new name. The new name is Israel, which means "wrestler with God." It is no accident that the homeland of the Jewish people and one of the names Christians have for their community is "Israel." I am suggesting that the only way to deal with the Bible is by wrestling with it, and that dislocated joints of various kinds may be part of the result.

Now I am not so foolish as to attempt to give you a summary of the whole Biblical narrative, but I must give you enough of a summary to show where the Ten Commandments fit. The story begins with a couple named Abraham and Sarah, who believe they have been called to leave a city which is one of the centers of civilization of that time. They are called to go with some relatives and associates to the remote area known today as Israel/Palestine, and to make a new life there. Over time, the God who calls them makes a covenant with them. They and their descendants will be his people, and he will be their God.

Wait! Doesn't the Bible begin with creation, and the flood and all that? Yes it does, but those first chapters are a kind of prologue to the story of Abraham, Sarah and their spiritual descendants. It is important to acknowledge the Creator, for it means that we are creatures, related to everything else in the universe. The other main point of the creation stories is that the Creator pronounced the creation good, and then rested. We will get to what that might mean for us when we get to the Fourth Commandment. The point of the prologue for the story as a whole is that human beings, who were given a special responsibility to care for the creation, messed things up. This led to their exile from the garden that is their first home and to the corruption of their relationships, even to murder. God's offer to Abraham and Sarah is part of God's way to begin setting things right, restoring again the goodness of creation and the human role in it. Now, let's go back to that story.

Jacob/Israel is the grandson of Abraham and Sarah. He has a lot of children, including twelve sons, with a few wives. (This is what the Bible presents as a "traditional family.") The next-to-youngest son, Joseph, is a favorite of his dad. His jealous older brothers secretly sell him into slavery. He ends up in Egypt, another center of civilization, where he becomes the Prime Minister. In a time of famine, his brothers come to him for help, not knowing who he is. He reconciles with them, and the whole family moves to Egypt. They prosper for a few generations; then a new king, worried about these immigrants, reduces them to slavery and finally orders all their male children killed. This king is obviously unaware of the power of women; because women, both Israelite and Egyptian, see to it that one of the slave children, Moses, not only survives but is raised in the royal palace.

When as a young man Moses protests against injustice, he has to flee to the desert. There he has an encounter with a mysterious presence who tells him to return to Egypt and lead his people out to freedom. Moses wants to know the name of the one who is calling him, but gets this strange response: "I AM WHO I AM. Do what I have asked you to do, and you will find out who I am." As with Abraham and Sarah, knowing God is possible only through undertaking a journey in faith, doing what God calls us to do.

So Moses goes, and the going is not easy. The king vacillates. Disasters fall on the land. Finally, the people miraculously make it into the desert with the leadership of Moses and his sister Miriam. So there they are, free at last . . . but in the desert! Just when they are starting to think that maybe they were better off as slaves in Egypt, they find themselves camped at the foot of a mountain which is behaving just like it was an active volcano. Moses is called to go up the mountain to meet the mysterious presence. There God tells Moses to remind the people of how he has liberated them, and to offer them a covenant in which, if they follow God's instruction, they will become "a priestly kingdom and a holy nation." He comes back down with this message, and the people agree to their part in this covenant. After one more trip up and down the mountain for Moses and his brother Aaron, there follows, in Exodus, chapter 20, the Ten Commandments, spoken by God.

The people hear the voice of God, but it is too much for them. They ask Moses to carry on listening to God, and then to tell them what was said. So Moses goes back into "the thick darkness where God was." What follows are eleven chapters of detailed instructions on a wide variety of topics, at the end of which God gives Moses ". . . the two tablets of the covenant, tablets of stone, written with the finger of God." Later we shall consider the fate of those stone tablets.

The "I AM" has offered a covenant to the people, just as with Abraham and Sarah. The Ten Commandments, God's contribution to the terms of this covenant, give the people the shape of freedom, but learning to live as free people takes the practice of faith and hope and love. It takes generations of wandering in the desert before the people finally, after the death of Moses, return to the land promised to Abraham and Sarah. Before Moses dies, he makes a great farewell speech to the people, reminding them of the covenant relationship at the heart of their freedom.

Another version of the Ten Commandments is included in Moses' final address to the people, found in chapter five of Deuteronomy (the name means "second law"). When we get to a discussion of the commandments, I will give the two versions of each commandment, so that we can reflect on the differences. One significant feature of the Bible is that it includes more than one version of many major topics (e.g., creation, the life of King David, the life of Jesus), as if to invite us to search for and be challenged by multiple perspectives and divergent interpretations.

After entering the Promised Land, the people struggle with their neighbors, often with bloody consequences. Eventually they make someone king, in spite of their previous bad experience with kings. Their second king is a man named David, a combination guerilla warrior and song-writer. His greatest hits are the core of the justly famous book of Psalms. For a brief synopsis of his character, consult Leonard Cohen's song, *Hallelujah*.

After King David and his successor son Solomon, the kingdom is divided. Many prophets arise to warn the people that they are not truly living the way of freedom in either their politics or religion. While their voices are treasured by some and remembered to this day, the Promised Land is eventually conquered by other, more powerful, kings and their armies. Eventually the great temple built by Solomon is destroyed, and the leaders of the people are taken away to exile in Babylon. After some generations, "I AM" continues to be faithful to the covenant, enabling the too-often-unfaithful people to return to the Promised Land and to rebuild the temple in Jerusalem, David's capital city. But true freedom is still elusive. The great empires of Persia, then Greece, then Rome include Israel in their domain, despite occasional rebellions.

For Christians, this story leads to its climax in the story of Jesus of Nazareth, paradoxically affirmed by Christians to be both fully human and truly the Incarnation of God, the Son of his Father. We see him as Messiah or Christ (that is, Anointed One or King, as David was). He lived to embody true human freedom, died showing us how faithful suffering exposes and overcomes injustice and oppression, and was raised from the dead to open the door of freedom for all people. His disciples (followers whose lives are disciplined—guided—by his teaching) are to be the agents of the freedom of God's covenant community until his return to complete God's liberating purpose, a fulfillment sometimes imagined as a New Jerusalem. These very human disciples and their community, fallible and fragile, can hope to experience this freedom and fulfill their part of the covenant only through the presence of the Holy Spirit, God freely living and active among and within these disciples. The unity of the "I AM"–Father, Son, and Holy Spirit–we call Trinity, while recognizing that human language is never able to express fully the mysterious presence.

The Christian story has too often been told in a way that makes it sound as if the story of the Israelites before Christ no longer matters. In this testimony, I understand the story to be one. The division between those Israelites now called Jews and those now called Christians, a division that has led to extremes of injustice and unimaginable human suffering, is a sign of the incompleteness of the story and a challenge to our capacity for hope. But the division does not prevent me from claiming my place in the story of covenant relationship with the God who wrestles with us and blesses us with commandments that give us the way toward freedom.

4

The First Commandment:
a faithful atheism

I am the Lord your God, who brought you out of the land of Egypt, out of the house of slavery; you shall have no other gods besides me.

EXODUS 20:2–3 AND DEUTERONOMY 5:6–7

THESE WORDS ARE SPOKEN to Moses on the very mountain where he had first encountered the mysterious presence. The story of that first encounter is told in Exodus 3. Having fled Egypt and begun a family in the desert, he now hears a voice from a fiery bush telling him to return to Egypt and lead his enslaved people, the Israelites, to freedom. "Who am I to do such a thing?" Moses asks. The answer is: "I will be with you; and this will be the sign for you that it is I who have sent you: when you have brought the people out of Egypt, you shall worship God on this mountain."

Now it seems obvious that such an answer is no answer at all. Moses is not given any superpowers, only faith. "When you have led my people to freedom, as I am calling you to do, and return with them to this place, you will know that you are the one to do it." As he follows this call to freedom, he will learn, step by step, that the one who is calling him is truly with him. When he returns to this place of calling, the next steps will be revealed. The path for these steps will be formed by the Commandments.

Moses is understandably not quite convinced by the answer of faith alone. Maybe he is okay to follow this path, but how will he convince the people? "If I tell them that the God of your ancestors has sent me, and they ask me "What is the name of this God?" What do I tell them?" Here is the answer, another answer that can be seen as no answer at all: God says to Moses, "I AM WHO I AM." He goes on to say that Moses should tell the Israelites, "I AM has sent me to you."

There are many names for God in the Bible. In fact, the Bible acknowledges the existence of many gods. One name of a god which occurs frequently is untranslated in most English Bibles as Ba'al. As I understand it, this name means something like "the Power," or maybe even "the Force." The Bible nowhere doubts the existence of such beings, and the first commandment has nothing to say about the theoretical question of their existence and, in fact, seems to assume that they do exist. The first commandment simply invokes the story of this people, their passage from slavery to freedom which began with the encounter between Moses and the mysterious presence on the mountain, and calls for the justice of acknowledging the initiative and continuing presence ("I will be with you") of the one who has brought them to this freedom.

On one hand, this presence has no name at all ("I AM WHO I AM"), and cannot be known as things, including the beings called gods, are known. On the other hand, this declaration gives a personal name, a name that sets this God apart from all others ("I AM"). Transliterated from Hebrew, this personal name is YHWH, or Yahweh. In many Jewish traditions, this name is so sacred that it is never to be said or written. I apologize to any Jewish friends who may be offended by my use of it here, and having done so for explanatory reasons, I promise not to do it again. Earlier versions of the English Bible sometimes mistakenly rendered the sacred name as "Jehovah," which is at least a personal name, although it lacks the power and intention of the Hebrew. More recent translations usually follow Jewish practice by writing "the Lord" whenever the sacred name would otherwise occur. There are problems with this, as "the Lord" is hardly a personal name; it does not adequately convey the particular historical context in which the name is given, and it sounds like the kind of name one might give to any of the other beings who have evoked human worship, such as Ba'al. But the God of the Bible is not a generic god, not one of the multitude from whose worship the Israelites are, by this commandment, forever set free.

Just to make it clear, I am saying that the shape of freedom given in the first commandment is freedom from the need to believe in any of the gods the world or human traditions set before us; freedom to be, in that sense, atheists. We are not free, when confronted by the mysterious presence and the call to justice, not to answer. Our pretending not to have heard that call does not allow us to evade answering; it only means that our answer is a refusal, either a "no" or a "not yet." That call may come in the form of direct experience, as it did for Moses, or in the form of the testimony of another, such as the one I hear and the one you are now reading. Even now, you are free to answer as your heart and soul and mind lead you to answer, but you are not free not to answer.

In what way, then, am I endorsing atheism? In one sense atheism is a rejection of theism, a philosophical stance which holds that the world and human experience can best be understood if one postulates the existence of one or more gods. This implies that the existence of this god or these gods can be demonstrated rationally. Theism would be more convincing if I AM had given Moses a different answer to the questions he asked, such as an actual name, like Zeus or Thor or The Market. I am not arguing that belief in God is irrational. In fact, it seems to me that the pursuit of scientific knowledge and philosophical wisdom makes the most sense if one is living out a biblical (Christian, Jewish, Muslim) faith. But that is another topic.

I am arguing from biblical evidence that the existence of the God of biblical faith cannot be "proved." Human reason cannot comprehend I AM. To prove the existence of something is to assume that "it" is a "thing." The mysterious presence who met Moses on the mountain, the I AM who brought the people out of slavery, the one whom Jesus prayed to as Abba/Our Father, the God of this story, is neither an "it" nor a "thing." To claim to prove the existence of this God is a demonstration of the intellectual pride and theological error of the one making the claim. If you can prove the existence of a god, it is not the God of biblical faith.

I am an atheist in a practical rather than a philosophical sense. It is not because I think the existence of such gods as The Market and Military Might (known by the Romans, for whom he was important, as Mars) cannot be shown to exist. In fact, their existence, and the existence of the cults by which they are worshipped is all too clear. I am an atheist because, as a Christian, the First Commandment sets me free from the need to worship such gods, or the need to acknowledge the reality behind them as anything other than one aspect of the way the world is now, a reality with which we all must deal one way or another, simple brute fact, something we can try to change.

So if I cannot demonstrate the existence of the God of Abraham and Sarah, of Moses and Miriam, of Jesus and his disciples, why do I claim to be a Christian? How can I be both an atheist and a believer? Like you, I have been confronted by a claim upon my life by the mysterious presence, a claim that comes to us from within ourselves and through others, a call to a life of freedom from the various forms of servitude the world as it now is offers us. The claim is that we can only know the true freedom being offered to us by walking faithfully, that is, with trust that, like Moses and the Israelites, we will experience truth and freedom as we journey together. That is why I say that the beginning of this journey towards freedom begins with the faithful atheism offered in the First Commandment, freedom from the gods of the world as it is, and from the sacrifices they inevitably require of us.

I offer three illustrations of these gods and their demands for sacrifice. First is the god we may call More, or, less elegantly, Stuff, or more provocatively, Capitalism. The heart of this heartless faith (apologies to K. Marx) is the belief that our happiness, and the true meaning of life, is to be found by making and possessing more of whatever can be possessed. The focus can be crude (money) or refined (works of art). Because More is a shape-shifter, money is usually the focus because it is widely, if falsely, considered to be convertible into anything else. But the basic doctrine is not that having lots of money is a good thing. Indeed, someone who has lots of money and is content to enjoy it is considered in this religion to be decadent or lazy, and doomed to insignificance. The imperative of this faith is always to be seeking to have More.

Do you have a place to sleep, some food each day, enough clothing to stay warm in most weather, but no more? You will be regarded as, at best, unfortunate; at worst, a disgrace and a drain on society. Do you have a home for yourself and your family? Others have larger, better furnished ones. You need to work harder or find a better job so that you can keep up to the ever-rising standard. Have you the economic resources to live your predictable life in relative comfort? If you invested more wisely and aggressively you could have more than you could ever possibly need, and leave more money to those who will inherit your estate. If you are a millionaire, you should be trying to become a billionaire. After all, the purpose of having wealth is . . . to make more wealth. One can never be too secure. These are small examples from within the most affluent society the world has ever seen.

Advertising is the art form invented within and peculiar to this religion. The purpose of all advertising is to persuade you that you need More, that your life could be better if you acquire what is being advertised. Advertising, to risk oversimplification, aims to make you feel either needy or smug. ("Good thing I already have/ use that!") Mad Men indeed.

The imperative of More can perhaps be better seen on a larger scale. The health of a nation's economy is judged by its rate of growth. A persistent negative rate of economic growth is called a depression, a kind of collective spiritual illness. Political parties across the spectrum are agreed that economic growth is the ulti- mate purpose of both commerce and government. Even political movements concerned about the environment assure us that a green economy will grow as well if not better than one based on resource depletion. Such is the power of More. The Biblical faiths–Judaism, Christianity, Islam–and the philosophers of ancient Greece were once agreed that greed was a common and serious human vice, a form of self-destructive behavior. The religion of More has succeeded in penetrating the human world to such an extent that today many who regard themselves as Christians, or Jews, or Muslims, or philosophers, actually regard the unlimited pursuit of More as a virtue rather than a vice. The lack of what was once called greed is regarded as a character flaw, the absence of ambition.

So where is the human sacrifice required by this powerful religion? On the personal level, it can be seen in the way the pursuit of More calls for the sacrifice of one's time and energy. The most "successful" must work almost incessantly. Advances in electronic communications make this both possible and, for true believers, unavoidable. There is little time for friends or family. Career is all-consuming. Instability of marriages and fragility of friendships are sacrifices willingly made. Happiness can never be achieved as, by definition, there is always More to be sought. We can see the sacrifice of happiness in our culture as people, urged on by advertising, give themselves to the discontent required by More. Suicide rates demonstrably increase among the devotees of More, and also among those (thinking now of the young people taking their own lives in remote indigenous communities in Canada) who, thanks to the media, can see More from a distance, but are not allowed to hope for participation in the cult.

Of course, there are ways developed by the religion of More for dealing with the impossibility of happiness. More, having led much of science into its service in the form of technology, gives us enhanced versions of the opioids which our bodies naturally produce to deal with stress. However, the worship of More supplemented by opioid consumption predictably leads to further human sacrifice, both among the true believers, for whom there can never be enough of anything, and especially from those who are forced to seek their pharmaceutical solace from unreliable sources.

Again, we can perhaps see this sacrifice most clearly on a global scale. More demands the destruction of the environment that makes human life possible, for that environment is seen as only a resource for More, and it is a finite environment. Some true believers try to avoid this problem by postulating the imperative of finding and moving to another planet or solar system or galaxy. Unfortunately, this is an imagined option only for those few closest to More. And the human race may survive the finitude of Planet Earth in an altered state, after "the Singularity." But in the short term, while we await the deliverance of the favored few, the lives of many more vulnerable human beings will be sacrificed to More through environmental degradation, along with other species of organic life, from coral reefs to tigers. The scope of this sacrifice will grow with the appetite of More.

A second illustration involves a lesser god, but one who nevertheless has many followers. We may call it Fame. We live in a world where freedom, and even reality, is located in individuals. Participation in a community may be desirable or not, depending on one's own aspirations. At best, community is seen as merely a means to the goals of the individuals who choose to participate; at worst it is an obstacle to self-realization, to be avoided whenever possible.

It is not surprising that, in such a world, people can wonder anxiously about whether they matter to anyone else. Such anxiety fuels our fascination with romantic love, as well as with its notorious transiency. We expect that "falling in love" will magically assure us that we matter to at least one other person. But since this bond is based on emotions that predictably fluctuate in individuals whose needs and desires may change, the magic of romantic love is unreliable and anxiety-producing. In the world of the isolated individual, I need more than the fragile devotion of one person to be sure that I truly matter. I need recognition from many. That is called fame, and Fame is another god requiring human sacrifice from its devotees.

Not that the worship of Fame is something new, emerging only in our individualistic culture. It appears that humans have always been tempted to do good things for the wrong reason, in this case so that they will become famous, recognized and admired by people, many of whom they will never know. It is surely a good thing to want to make beautiful things, or sing and play beautiful songs, or discover previously unknown facts, or to perform excellently in a sport, or to do anything that improves the quality of human life. The worship of the god Fame distorts these good ambitions by making the ones attempting them forget why they are doing it. I might be writing this essay in order to help myself and my readers understand something better; but when I worship Fame I forget that purpose and try to write instead whatever will attract the attention of the most possible readers, or whatever circle of readers or Facebook or Twitter or Snapchat followers I want to impress. I might try to condition my body so that I can do my very best in some athletic event; but when I worship the god Fame I will do anything to win, to set a new record. That might well include cheating or taking performance-enhancing drugs. I might want to serve my community by being elected to public office; but when I worship the god Fame I forget serving the community and concentrate on being elected or re-elected, whatever I might have to say or do to accomplish that.

Just as the god More turned greed into a virtue, the god Fame has recently turned idolatry into something that seems desirable. We now have contests to see who can become an "idol" of one sort or another. Well, what is wrong with that? The answer becomes clearer when we remember that an idol, in the original sense of the word, is an image. Fame requires those who would become famous to become (we say "project") an image that will find a place in the imagination of the multitudes. To be famous in this way, I must pretend to be someone I am not. It is my image that will be famous. Genuine recognition and admiration comes from others who know a person whose life is making the world a better place. That person may be famous to some degree, but because they have not worshipped the god Fame they are still themselves. Their fame does not depend upon the easily changeable imagination of multitudes who will never know them as they truly are.

The surrender of the self to an image is the human sacrifice demanded by the god Fame. The one who becomes famous in this way becomes more image than reality. Without pretending that I can know or truly judge them, and without diminishing their genuine gifts and achievements, it appears that lives such as those of Michael Jackson and Marilyn Monroe illustrate the extent of the sacrifice which Fame may require. It is sobering to realize that many people yearn to follow the same path.

Our third example is all too obvious in our world, and that is our trust in violence or the threat of violence to keep us safe. Let us use the Roman name and call it Mars. Despite my parents' best intentions, I was taught this faith from childhood. The cowboy movies I saw almost every week, combined with Tom Mix and The Lone Ranger on the radio, showed me that a good guy with a gun could overcome the evil in the world, usually by killing one or more bad guys. This imaginary world existed within the real world of the Second World War, in which the undoubted evil of Hitler and his allies could only be brought to an end by using weapons of mass destruction (that "mass" included a lot of non-combatant human beings) before or more effectively than the enemy could.

The experience of that war, despite the staggering human sacrifices taken by Mars, did not turn the human race away from its worship. Resources devoted to Mars have only increased, as has our fear. First our ally, the Soviet Union, became our enemy, and then the Cold War brought on the possibility of nuclear war. Now the prospect of a petty dictator lobbing missiles in the general direction of Alaska calls for further acts of worship, that is, human sacrifice.

Such is the worship of Mars on the global scene. But the worship of Mars on a personal level also requires human sacrifice. This religion is based on fear, and too often we are fearful of some of those we encounter in our daily life. When we choose to defend ourselves by pre-emptive violence, or encourage our law enforcement officers to do so on our behalf, we allow our fear to control our lives and fragment our communities. Mars requires human sacrifice, not just of our enemies, but also of us. This is not to deny that strength is required in the defense of justice. But real strength cannot be found in a world ruled by fear, a world where Mars is worshipped. The First Commandment frees us from the worship of Mars, and thus empowers us to seek the real strength which comes from courageously seeking justice.

Many other examples could be given. We have shown an astounding capacity to take elements of life (wealth, fame, strength, sexual relations, etc.), none of which are evil in themselves, and turn them into objects of worship, gods to whom we sacrifice ourselves and others. The First Commandment offers us a way to walk in freedom from these gods, and to enjoy the gifts of the real world that I AM, the creator and liberator, puts before us.

5

The Second Commandment: freedom for imagination

You shall not make for yourself an idol, whether in the form of anything that is in heaven above, or that is on the earth beneath, or that is in the water under the earth. You shall not bow down to them or worship them; for I the Lord your God am a jealous God, punishing children for the iniquity of parents, to the third and fourth generation of those who reject me, but showing steadfast love to the thousandth generation of those who love me and keep my commandments.

EXODUS 20:4–6 AND DEUTERONOMY 5:8–10

IF TECHNICAL STUFF BORES you, skip to the next paragraph. This is where we acknowledge that there is more than one way to number the Ten Commandments. You can see for yourself how the verses above can easily be seen as a continuation of the First

Commandment. The tradition of Roman Catholics and Lutherans counts these verses as part of number one, and divides what we will treat as number ten into two parts. In this writing, I will be following the tradition of Jews and the kind of Protestant Christians who first nurtured my faith. I am not inclined to argue with anyone about this. Maybe we should call them the Nine Commandments, or the Eleven Commandments. But for now, let's stick with ten, which brings us to the topic of numbers in the Bible. Often the numbers are symbolic rather than literal. Probably the best example is the story about creation happening in seven days. To take this number literally is absurd and disrespectful of the text. Seven is used as a perfect, complete number, based on the number of days in the week, which is itself the length of one phase of the moon. We will think more about this when we get to the Fourth Commandment. Another example is the number 40. The Israelites spent 40 years in the wilderness at the beginning of their freedom from slavery; Jesus spent 40 days in the wilderness at the beginning of his liberating work. The use of 40 in the latter story obviously means to connect it with the former story. In both stories it means an extended time of preparation. In neither story is it intended literally. We could look at many more examples, but let's get back to the Second Commandment (apologies to my Catholic and Lutheran friends), noticing as we do that human beings normally have ten fingers, thus helping us remember the commandments.

If the words "You shall not make for yourself an idol." are not to be taken as merely an elaboration of the First Commandment, we will need to focus on what might be meant by "making an idol." Often this has been taken as meaning a visual representation of some god, a painting or sculpture or something of that sort. There have been some spectacular, fatality-causing disagreements between Christians over the use of visual art and sculpture in public and private worship. Those who disapproved—the original iconoclasts—felt that these icons were forbidden by this commandment. The iconophiles have tended to prevail among Christians, while the iconoclasts have been dominant in Islam.

I want to suggest another approach to this commandment, one that will leave this long debate over the place of the arts in

Christian life unresolved, but which will encourage us to see what a challenge the commandment presents to us, whatever our view of the historic debate. Suppose that making an idol refers not just to the work of our hands, but to that which lies behind the work, to our thoughts and words as well. What if it refers to our imagination? What if I AM is beyond our imagination, and any product of our imagination we claim as a god, or even as God, is potentially an idol? What does this mean for what is called "organized religion?" And how does keeping this commandment set us on the path to faithful freedom?

Earlier I promised that we would return to the story of the tablets of stone. Chapter 32 of Exodus contains a wonderful story that tells what happened to them while perfectly illustrating the role of imagination in idolatry. All those eleven chapters of additional laws took a long time to receive, it seems, for Moses was on the mountain for (You guessed it!) 40 days. Moses' brother Aaron has been left in charge down below. Now 40 days can seem like a long time, especially in the desert. The people grow anxious and restless. Who knows what has happened to Moses up there, with all that smoke and thunder? We need someone who will show us the way!

Aaron does not handle this anxiety well. He thinks he has to *do something*. Here are the steps his imagination takes: first, let's gather all our gold. What good is gold in the desert, anyway? You can't eat or drink it. Then let's make a reassuring image with this gold, maybe something that suggests a source of food, maybe a calf. You know, you can drink the milk and eat the cheese and then make burgers. This statue will look good and suggest prosperity, the kind we saw from a distance in Egypt. Then we can have a big party, and maybe folks can enjoy themselves and forget about their anxiety and get off my back, at least for a while.

Aaron's imagination works in the short term, in spite of the fact that they have already been given the Ten Commandments, which they seem to have forgotten already. But when Moses arrives with the stone tablets, all hell breaks loose, Moses breaks the tablets, destroys the golden calf, and makes the people drink water in which the ground-up gold has been dissolved. Then the following dialogue ensues (Exodus 32:21-24):

Moses said to Aaron, What did this people do to you that you have brought so great a sin upon them?" (Moses is offering his brother Aaron a way to excuse himself, and Aaron takes it gratefully.) *And Aaron said, "Do not let the anger of my lord burn hot; you know the people, that they are bent on evil. They said to me, "Make us gods, who shall go before us; as for this Moses, the man who brought us up out of the land of Egypt, we do not know what has become of him." So I said to them, "Whoever has gold, take it off; so they gave it to me, and I threw it into the fire, and out came this calf!"*

When we have stopped laughing at the outrageous comedy of this last line, we can ponder what the story tells us about idolatry. First there is the role of anxiety. There were lots of gods and, as we know, lots of world-class art and artifacts in Egypt. Think of pyramids and mummies and the Sphinx. But we were slaves there, and we longed for freedom. Now we are free, and wondering why it is taking so long—40 days . . . 40 years!—to get our life together. The people who enslaved us seemed to have a great life, so let's try to be more like them.

When I review this story, I am reminded of my Welsh ancestors who had become virtually enslaved by the English landlords and factory owners during the Industrial Revolution. Many left for North America, the land of freedom, where all too many ended up becoming . . . slave owners. It seems that we do not often learn justice from experiencing oppression. We are more likely to learn how to oppress others. The transition from slavery to freedom is not easy. A life of slavery leaves marks that can only be removed as we, patiently and diligently, receive the gift of freedom and discern the path that we, as free people, must walk. In our confusing world, we have many examples to follow. The famous, the rich, the strong, the dominant are always before us. It is easy to try to follow their example, but hard to find our own way. In our anxiety to succeed, it is always tempting to follow the example of the very people who make us feel anxious. Freedom, in contrast, is not something we achieve for ourselves. It comes as a gift, free but not easy, just as it was given to the Israelites.

Then there is that precious but dangerous human capacity, imagination. Without imagination, we have no future and no world. Even those who encourage us to "live in the moment" rely on imagination to construct a sense of living and the notion of a "moment." Imagination is surely one of the greatest gifts given to our species. But anxiety can do terrible things to our imagination. It opens us to the temptation to regard the products of our imagination as having a life of their own, as in "I threw it into the fire, and out came this calf." Once we give in to the temptation, we are no longer responsible for its product. It just *is*, and we now give ourselves the right to expect others to regard it so. Notice the three-fold effect: I no longer take responsibility *for* what I have imagined; in fact, I now find myself responsible *to* it, since it has an existence independent of me; and I assume the right to impose what I have imagined *upon* others, since I assume it is as real for them as it is for me. When the human imagination operates in this way, as an agent of enslavement, we may properly call it idolatry.

These connections help us understand what otherwise seems very harsh about this commandment. "Punishing children for the iniquity of parents" sounds vindictive, as if God gets really mad if we do not follow the rules. But what if this is not meant to be prescriptive, but descriptive? We give to our children our sense of how the world is, and must be. When we walk the path of freedom, we share that freedom with those around us. When we worship and yield our freedom to the constructs of our fear-driven, anxious imagination, the result is contagious. The social constructs that limit our lives, such as racism, nationalism, patriarchy, and homophobia are forms of idolatry, spiritual illnesses that are readily transmitted. The Second Commandment calls us to walk away from them toward freedom and "steadfast love."

Now we return to the second of our original questions. What does this commandment mean for our understanding of "organized religion?" Some folks like to say that they are "spiritual" but not "religious." I believe they mean that in their search for an adequate sense of the meaning and purpose of life they have not found participation in formally constituted communities of faith helpful or worthwhile. I also believe that, in saying this, these folks are expressing inadequately but understandably what the second commandment is all about. They are noticing that, on the path of freedom, community can sometimes be more hindrance than help. This is surely true of all kinds of community. There are dysfunctional families who inflict terrible wounds on one another. There are friendships which are narrowing and destructive in the sense that they shut out, even belittle or attack, those outside the circle of friendship. There are nations in which patriotism comes to mean the building of walls and the constant threat of war. And there are churches (also synagogues, mosques, gurdwaras, cults, etc.) in which the life of faith becomes moralistic and judgmental, and in which active, critical thinking is discouraged and imagination is frozen.

This does not mean that that all forms of community are bad, or that the path of freedom involves the avoidance of community. Family and friendship are essential to human good; I believe Aristotle was right when he said that humans are political animals. These are dimensions of human life which need to be redeemed, not avoided. This is not to deny the tragic fact that all forms of community, including churches, can go terribly wrong. The capacity for life together is one of the great gifts to human beings, just as is imagination. And, as with imagination, anxiety (or fear, ignorance, greed, etc.) can take it down the path of slavery. What the "spiritual but not religious" folks are seeing, and calling "organized religion" is the path of slavery. What I want us to see is the possibility of freedom.

Religious communities can become idols. The Protestant Reformation rejected the idolatry it saw in the Roman Catholic Church, but the ensuing religious warfare led some Protestants to make idols of the Bible as they imagined it, or of doctrines telling us how to interpret the Bible. I have seen churches make idols of popularity, adherence to organizational rules, and forms of "political correctness." In each case, possibilities for freedom are lost.

The Second Commandment, then, shows us the path by which we can enjoy our freedom while remaining open to the joys and struggles of life-in-community, including communities of faith. Like Moses, we have the mandate to challenge the idolatry of religious institutions while continuing, like Moses with Aaron, to be a good sister or brother to those with whom we share those joys and struggles. Even freedom can be imagined as an idol. When we imagine our freedom as a possession to be grasped and defended against others, as something that belongs to us as solitary individuals, we have truly lost our way. Freedom is a path to be walked with others, shared with others as they both nurture and challenge us. It is a gift to the "children of Israel," and it is offered to us as we participate in our families, our friendships, our political communities, and our communities of faith.

6

The Third Commandment:
freedom for listening

You shall not make wrongful use of the name of the
Lord your God, for the Lord will not acquit anyone who
misuses his name.

EXODUS 20:7 AND DEUTERONOMY 5:11

AT THE TIME OF this writing, a minister of the United Church of
Canada is making some others in that communion uneasy by arguing that the church can perform its ministry better by not talking
about God. Of course, this puts her at odds with the statements
of faith which define the church. Unitarian Universalists, a few of
whom I know and respect deeply, would find her position agree-
able; but she seems less interested in finding the fellowship of the
like-minded than in challenging her United Church brothers and
sisters to think about what they are saying. Since I am here encouraging the reader to take seriously the faith of Abraham, Moses and

Jesus, I am not going to avoid writing about their God, the One whose biblical name is I AM. But I think my disturbing sister has a point, and it is exactly the point of the Third Commandment.

In a culture where we are led to believe we are secular, we talk about God with surprising frequency. Everyone knows what OMG means, although it is never clear which god is mine. "God" is regularly summoned to condemn things of which the speaker disapproves, whether seriously or frivolously. And no major political speech in the USA is complete without summoning some deity, often assumed to be the God of the Bible, to "bless America." All these are violations of the commandment, although the freedom which is lost in the violation is often no more, but surely no less, than the freedom to express oneself clearly. But to see the fuller intent of the commandment, to grasp the challenge involved in keeping it, and to become aware of the freedom offered by the keeping of it, we must reflect on what it might mean for a community of faith to "make wrongful use" of the Name. The careless use of the word "god" outside of the covenant community is trivial in its consequences compared to the misuse of the language of faith within that community and its life in relation to the world. Let us examine some typical ways in which the name is misused, along with the consequences of this misuse, so we may see how this commandment leads us toward freedom.

First, there is the way in which "God" (I am using the word in quotation marks to point to the use of a word in the English language.) is used as a weapon against perceived enemies, as an excuse to denigrate, oppress or kill people of other nationalities, religions, or even other varieties of our own faith. Christians have a wretched record when it comes to this commandment. Not that other faith groups do not do similar things; but surely those who claim the covenant of which this commandment is a part have no valid excuse here. We will raise related matters when we reach the Sixth Commandment, but here the issue is the way "God" is used to justify hostility. Once "God" is invoked, the hostility is irreversible. If I do this because it is the will of "God," I can no longer examine my attitude or behavior critically. I can no longer admit to my mistakes or my brokenness and ask for forgiveness. A change in the relationship is no longer possible. I am locked into a hostile relationship unless or until I can acknowledge that I have broken the commandment, that the One I call "God" has not been "on my side," and that I have misused the name.

Second, there is the way "God" is invoked to control the behavior of others. This can be done with a good conscience, but out of anxiety. Examples: My child seems to be headed down the wrong path; only the fear of "God" can bring the needed correction. Social practices are changing in a way we find unsettling; "God" is invoked to steer our moral sense back to the traditions which have shaped us. The aboriginal people on whose lands we have settled have practices and wisdom which are strange to us. The dispossession we have caused has made their life more difficult. We are prospering while they are impoverished and too often in despair. If only they could be more "like us." "God," in the form of our culture and morality, has blessed us. So let us establish residential schools in which they can be taught the way of "God," and their own culture extinguished.

These are examples of the way that "God" can be made to serve our moralism. Morality is good. It is the attempt we make to lead the best kind of lives we can. Moralism is the attempt to impose our morality upon others. Moralism in the name of "God" is the attempt to paint my own sense of moral judgment with a cosmic coat, presenting it to others—and to ourselves—as something more than the effort of the fallible being I am. Moralism in the name of "God" is the enemy of freedom. It is the attempt, usually unsuccessful, to restrict the freedom of others to find their own way, to see their brokenness and find healing in their own way. Ironically, when I invoke "God" in support of my moralizing, I also restrict my own freedom. Condemning the behavior of others in the name of "God" is like throwing a boomerang; the standard I have set is now the one by which I shall be judged. It is no wonder that moralism in the name of "God" is rejected as hypocrisy.

Finally, there is the way that God-talk can trivialize our thinking and our imagination about the source of meaning and purpose in our lives. We have looked at the political and moral dimensions of the Third Commandment. Now we come to the theological dimension. Here I can only proceed by running the risk of contradicting myself; for theology is talk about God by fallible human beings, and such talk is always in danger of misusing the name. Let the reader beware.

The problem is that theology tries to put into words the Mysterious Presence who is beyond our understanding, to name the One who is beyond our language and our thought. Our only justification for theology is that the One we call God has invited us to this task, has "revealed himself," as we awkwardly say, already stumbling over the limits of a language in which persons are gendered. We can only undertake theology because of our stories. So we have reason to speak of the God of Abraham and Sarah and their descendants the Israelites, the God who confronted Moses as "I AM," the God who led us out of slavery, the God who made covenant with us at Mount Sinai, the God who brought us into the Promised Land, the God who brought us back from exile, the God who became one of us in the life and death of Jesus of Nazareth, the God who defeated the forces of evil and death through Jesus' resurrection, the God whose Spirit lives in and through us by faith, the God who calls us to live our lives as instruments of love. Our talk about God, our theology, is legitimate only as long as it remains rooted in this story and its claim upon our lives. Apart from that story, our talk about God is "a noisy gong or a clanging cymbal," and a violation of the Third Commandment. Apart from the story and its claim upon us, the Mysterious Presence refutes our names, and our God-talk is blasphemous.

So what freedom does the commandment offer us? Clearly, the story just outlined is not the only story people live by. Stories that tell us who we are and what makes life worth living abound in our global culture. Judaism and Islam offer significant alternatives to the Christian story. Asian cultures offer stories and what we might call God-talk that has been shown to have global reach and relevance. Stories from indigenous cultures offer deep wisdom rooted in the experience of life in particular places. Those who have come to share those places ignore these stories at their peril. The sciences and technology of the modern world have generated narratives that shape our lives, even when the bearers of these stories present them as simply "the facts." The Third Commandment, warning us against abstracting our God-talk from our particular story, offers us a sense of humility. We know nothing about God apart from our story. We have the freedom to share our story with others in the humbling awareness of the limits of our knowledge and our language, and we have the blessed freedom to listen respectfully to the stories of our near and distant neighbors, and to learn from them whatever helps us understand and appreciate them and our world more fully.

If Christians, even troublesome United Church ministers, decide to be much more careful in the way they talk about God, perhaps even suspending God-talk for a season of repentance, we can be grateful that they are, whether they know it or not, encouraging us to heed the warning and enjoy the freedom of the Third Commandment.

7

The Fourth Commandment: freedom to rest and enjoy

*Remember the Sabbath day and keep it holy. Six days
you shall labor and do all your work. But the seventh
day is a Sabbath to the Lord your God; you shall
not do any work—you, your son or your daughter,
your male or female slave, your livestock, or the alien
resident in your towns. For in six days the Lord made
heaven and earth, the sea, and all that is in them, but
rested the seventh day; therefore the Lord blessed the
seventh day and consecrated it.*

EXODUS 20:8–11

*Observe the Sabbath day and keep it holy, as the Lord
your God commanded you. Six days you shall labor
and do all your work. But the seventh day is a Sabbath*

to the Lord your God; you shall not do any work—
you, or your son or your daughter, or your male or
female slave, or your ox or your donkey, or any of
your livestock, or the resident alien in your towns, so
that your male and female slave may rest as well as
you. Remember that you were a slave in the land of
Egypt, and the Lord your God brought you out from
there with a mighty hand and an outstretched arm;
therefore the Lord your God commanded you to keep
the Sabbath day.

DEUTERONOMY 5:12–15

WITH THIS COMMANDMENT WE reach the pivot-point in our path toward freedom. The first three point upwards, toward the One who has "brought us . . . out of the house of bondage." No other gods; no idols; no loose or malicious god-talk. The remaining six point outward, toward our neighbors. This fourth one looks both ways; so it is good that we have two versions, with Exodus reminding us of God's creative acts and Deuteronomy reminding us of our liberation from slavery. The day of rest (for that is what the Hebrew word translated as "Sabbath" means) honors both these gifts of God. The freedom of a day of rest is not just for me. I am obliged to share that freedom with my family, my employees, the immigrants who live in my community, and any animals for whom I am responsible. This gift is to be shared as widely as possible.

Seeing the Sabbath as a liberating gift lets us see what was wrong about the way some puritanical Christians have understood this commandment. In the town where I was raised, the big issue about the Sabbath was what you could not do. Some of our local Christians insisted that keeping Sabbath meant no playing cards, no baseball, and certainly no dancing; in other words, no fun. Defining the day of rest in such a way brought the sense of what it meant to be religious into general disrepute among my contemporaries. Sabbath was understood as a time when we were expected to be serious and wear less comfortable clothes. I hated the feel of those Sunday pants, and yearned for the return of the days of blue jeans.

Nothing could be further from the intention of this commandment. Yes, life involves work. There is the labor of the things that need to be done over and over: meals to be made, the house to be cleaned, snow to be shoveled, etc. This is labor we need to share with one another in a regular, reliable way. And there is work to be done. Whether through paid employment or not, our neighbors have needs that we are obliged to do our share in meeting. "Six days (that is, most of the time) you shall labor and do all your work." This is the life for which God has set us free. But that is not all there is to life. Sabbath is our way of remembering this truth.

As we have seen, the two versions of the commandment differ from each other mainly in the reason given for the commandment. The difference enriches the meaning of the commandment and the scope of the freedom to which it points. In Exodus, the Israelites have recently escaped from slavery in Egypt. They remember it clearly. But here they are in the desert, living day-to-day, while the Egypt they remember, with its massive buildings and impressive displays of power and wealth, are also remembered clearly. The Exodus version of the commandment calls us to be aware of the deeper reality, the reality of creation itself. God knows how to work, for all that exists comes from God's loving work. But the point of working is to enjoy the result. When God had finished the original work of creation, God rested and enjoyed the goodness of that amazing created universe. Work is good; it can even be fun. But the purpose of work is so that we can share with our neighbors in the pure enjoyment of this beautiful world.

Now one of the ideas passing as truth these days is that we humans are the creators of the world, and that our work is therefore never done. There is some truth in the idea that we are called to share in God's loving creativity, but the idea that it is all up to us and that we can make the world into anything we wish is a well-disguised invitation to return to slavery. Notice all the stores open 24/7. Notice who has to work all those late shifts, and those who have to do their shopping then. Notice the people who "have to" leave their electronic devices on all the time, even those who are not being paid to do so. Look in their faces, and you will see people whose lives are no longer their own, even if their slavery is well paid. They are in the modern version of biblical Egypt. The Exodus version of the commandment calling us to a day of rest reminds us that the point of living is not working or shopping or doing any of the things we think we "have to do," but the enjoyment that comes when we rest and celebrate the goodness of creation with those we love.

In contrast, the setting of Deuteronomy is at the end of the journey toward the Promised Land. Moses is about to die; most of those who left Egypt with him are dead. After forty years, the time of transition and preparation, most of the Israelites do not remember being slaves in Egypt. Moses makes one last, great speech to them before he dies. He wants to prepare them for what lies ahead—life in a land where the people live by the same rules as the Egyptians. There is wealth controlled by a few for their own benefit. There are religious and cultural practices designed to keep the masses impressed and amused. There are kings like Pharaoh, and eventually the Israelites will want one also, leading eventually to the kinds of practices that the prophets will have to denounce for their idolatry and corruption. Moses sees it coming, and knows the danger of the people forgetting their heritage of freedom, the danger that in their forgetfulness they will "return to Egypt" and slavery. So the commandment here reminds the people of how God gave them the gift of freedom. "Observe the Sabbath" when you enter this Promised Land as a way of remembering that you were slaves, and that God has given you freedom. And remember that this freedom is meant for everyone, including your employees and the immigrants living in your community, because once you were slaves and then refugees.

That is the promise of the Fourth Commandment. So work hard, but do not become a slave to your work or your career. Take time to enjoy the goodness of creation and have fun. Take time to remember the gifts you have been given, and be thankful.

And, as much as you can, share that joy and gratitude with your neighbors, near and far. This also is what God expects of us in response to the gift of freedom.[1]

---

1. Now for the only footnote in this writing: if you would like a deep and passionate take on the Fourth Commandment and why it is central to the path toward freedom, read Walter Brueggemann, *The Sabbath as Resistance: Saying No to the Culture of Now*, published by Westminster John Knox in 2014.

8

The Fifth Commandment: freedom to be yourself

Honor your father and your mother, so that your days may be long in the land that the Lord your God is giving you.

EXODUS 20: 12

NOW WE TURN TO the commandments that have to do with our relationship to our neighbors. The version in Deuteronomy 5 adds the words: "... *so that it may go well with you in the land that the Lord your God is giving you*" to the commandment, as if Moses wanted the people to remember that quality of life matters as much as length of life. Nothing affects the quality of our life more obviously than how we relate to our neighbors, especially those neighbors closest to us, that is, our family.

In my experience, there are no perfect families. Each one is broken in its own way. The hurts and disappointments we experience from our family members leave their scars on us, often much more deeply than the wounds which come from our more distant neighbors. It is from family that we expect love, and when that expectation is broken, our own ability to love and be loved is challenged. So this commandment may seem almost impossible to some folks, while others may mistakenly think that it is easy to do. As I am one of the latter, let us begin there.

On the surface, I appear to have had a perfect childhood. I was never in any doubt that my parents loved me. I never lacked for any necessity. Discipline was always administered firmly but calmly and without violence, although my mother and I had some spectacular fights when puberty and menopause arrived in our family simultaneously. Perhaps some of my flaws can be traced to being an only child, but that was the result of a late marriage, not my parents' choice. And there was a downside to being the child of the school Principal, later Superintendent of Schools in a small town, although it may sometimes have saved me from the physical consequences of my lack of diplomacy with my fellow students. So it must be easy to honor such parents, right?

Not really! What is easy is to yield to the temptation to idolize them. In our small town both my parents were highly respected. At my father's funeral a man who knew him well described him to me as . . . "the most honest man I have ever known." I heard it as a judgment on my own obviously deficient character. I knew, in that vulnerable moment, that I could never live up to such an example. When we put romanticized images of our parents on a pedestal, we cannot honor them, for we can never live up to the image. The worms of guilt and inadequacy—in my case, the sense of lacking integrity (father) and both musical and athletic ability (mother)—begin to eat the soul. These worms do not empower us to be our best selves. Rather, they lead us into self-deception, or despair, or both.

To truly honor our parents leads us toward respecting the truth about them, as well as we can know it, and to acknowledging the wounds as well as the gifts that made them who they are or were. To honor my father involves being aware that his mother died as he was born, that his beloved step-mother died from tuberculosis when he was a boy, that he had to leave home and live with his mother's relatives in order to attend high school, that it took many years to work his way through college, and that all these left wounds which made it very difficult for him to show affection to his privileged son. To honor my mother involves being aware that, when she was in her teens, her mother was consigned to a mental hospital where she eventually died, that as the eldest and only female of four children she was compelled to take on the domestic tasks of a mother, that the cultural assumptions of the day forced her to choose between life as a professional musician and life as a wife and a mother, and that somewhere in the process she lost the capacity to show affection by touching. For me to honor my father involves repentance for the pain my casual approach to academic work caused him who had worked so hard for his education. For me to honor my mother means embracing the changes in female-male relationships which feminism has brought about in our culture, not only because they are just, but also as a way of honoring the sacrifices my mother made.

We have put off looking at what is probably the more difficult problem. How does one honor a parent who has been a disappointment, or who has not taken the trouble to be part of their child's life? As I have not been in this position, my thoughts on this question are offered with great reservation. If they are offensive to anyone who reads them, I apologize.

The most obvious thing we can say about our parents is that they gave us life, whatever else came with the gift. Johnny Cash's great song, *A Boy Named Sue*, expresses this kind of honoring in an unforgettable way. We may want to kill the sonofa*#@^! who made our life so hard, but still that hard life and the toughness we have learned from it are a gift, with a peculiar beauty we can celebrate. There is something to be said for having the brokenness of life right there on the surface, where we cannot deny it, but rather must choose to learn from it or give in to it.

Of course, there are families in which the neglect, or abuse, suffered by someone at the hands of their family are not remotely related to the tongue-in-cheek affront captured in Johnny Cash's song. It can take a very long time, if ever, for such individuals to find anything in their families to honor or respect. But it is still the case that whatever resiliency, whatever courage, such individuals have, it had to come from somewhere. It is part of the legacy they have received, reflecting some mix of genetics and childhood experiences that stand in opposition to the shadow side of their heritage.

Another gift to us from the deficiencies of our parents is the opportunity to name and understand that deficiency, and to try not to replicate it in our own parenting. This is not an easy gift to receive, for too often we take for granted patterns of parenting learned in our childhood. Honoring our parents may mean careful reflection upon things that made our childhood difficult or painful, and a resolve to find better ways in our own parenting. I believe with gratitude that my own children have honored me and their mother in this way.

However, doing this is not just a matter of doing the opposite of what our parents did. If they were too strict, for example, it may not be helpful for us to forsake the discipline of our children altogether. Honoring our parents will involve the more difficult path of trying to understand why they chose the way they took, identifying what was valid in what they were trying to do, and discerning how what was good in them might be lived in a better way. I am not under the illusion that what I am suggesting here is easy, or that it can be accomplished without help. But I do want to insist that parents cannot be neatly divided into "good" and "bad," with the former to be honored and the latter cursed. All parents are flawed human beings, and we are called to honor them as they are or were, honestly naming, as well as possible, both their brokenness and the gifts they have given us.

There are strong voices in our world telling us that freedom involves distancing ourselves from our parents, leaving our past and our community of origin behind, and finding our true and unique selves. I believe this vision of selfhood and freedom to be profoundly inadequate. Before I argue that point further, I want to recognize what is true about it. It is an important step in the dance of life. The Parable of the Prodigal Son in Luke's Gospel is a portrayal of this dance. The younger brother, far from honoring his father, demands his share of the estate from the father and then takes off for a "far country." Having come face-to-face with his own brokenness there, he returns to his home and is welcomed by the father whom he has failed to honor . . . with celebration! He had to leave home, it seems, in order to find himself and his true home. The older son, who never left home, finds only bitter resentment. Honoring our parents does not mean remaining a child forever. Even if our parents have been totally inadequate, we will never find ourselves as long as we are merely victims of that inadequacy. In order to find ourselves and truly honor our parents, we must first find our own life, brokenness and all.

The gift of freedom to be yourself cannot be found by isolating yourself from your family, your roots. Leaving home can be a step in that direction, but to truly find yourself you must eventually come home, not necessarily in a literal or geographic sense, but in the sense of knowing where you come from, coming to terms with—and in that way honoring—those through whom God gave you the gift of life. Who you are is not some one thing given by fate or accident, nor is it something you determine for yourself and achieve by willing or dreaming it so. It is a gift given through your roots and shaped by how you walk the journey and dance the steps of your life. That journey begins with our relationship to our parents. To honor them is neither simple nor easy, but it is our first step toward the freedom to be ourselves.

9

The Sixth Commandment:
freedom for life together

You shall not murder.

EXODUS 20:13 AND DEUTERONOMY 5:17

THE MOST BASIC PROBLEM in understanding and responding to any message is discerning the meaning of the words. In the case of an ancient text such as the Bible, that problem is magnified. We have already seen an example of this problem in a matter as basic as the meaning of the biblical name for the God of the Israelites, the people of the path toward freedom. But now we have come to the Sixth Commandment, and are confronted with a question about its meaning which hinges on a single word. It is a problem Christians have never fully resolved for themselves, and so we must recognize the problem and accept its continuing existence.

"Murder," says the New Revised Standard Version and other recent and widely used translations. The King James Bible says, "kill." It seems, on the surface, that not murdering is fairly simple,

51

a commandment most of us apparently keep. But if we are commanded not to kill, does that mean we must be vegans, pacifists, and opposed to the death penalty and medical assistance in dying? There are Christians who have made a strong case for one or more of these interpretations, usually not all at once. What about the Hebrew word? I am no Hebrew scholar, but I am aware that there is some debate among scholars about the translation.

Having recognized the scope of the problem, let us take the simpler path. Let's assume that the modern translations are correct. After all, Torah clearly offers instructions about the slaughter of animals and the causes for which persons should be "put to death" by the community, as well as recording times when God directed the Israelites to engage in war. So, at least in those times and places and for those people, we can assume the narrow meaning while anticipating that it may get more complicated as we go along. What is involved in the commandment not to murder, and how does it lead us on the path toward freedom?

We might think it not necessary to command people not to kill. All it takes to restrain us is the recognition that the other person is a human being like us, given the gift of life in the same way we have been given it. So why does it happen? Why does one of us murder another?

Anger is one reason. Another person has done something which hurts us to our core, and we strike out at them in rage, a rage which might have been building up for a long time and which might be fueled in its energy and lack of restraint by alcohol, drugs or emotional illness. Is the commandment telling us that we should never be angry?

No, anger is a natural human emotion, given to us as a source of energy to help us make our world a better place. Combined with our ability to think, to calculate the effect of our actions, anger is a wonderful resource in overcoming injustice. When we supress our anger, bottle it up inside until it overpowers our ability to think clearly, we are on the way toward murder. "Do not let the sun go down on your anger" is good advice. In other words, deal with the situation while the energy of anger and your ability to think clearly can best work together. Confront the situation while you, rather than your anger, are in charge. The commandment frees us to receive anger as a gift, not a curse.

Closely related to anger as a reason for murder is revenge. Someone has taken the life, either directly or indirectly, of someone for whose well-being we consider ourselves responsible, and we act in response. There is a saying that revenge is "a dish best served cold." When someone is murdered as an act of revenge, the killer's ability to think, plan and calculate is not set aside, as when anger drives us. Rather, our reasoning power becomes crucial to the act. The murderer who kills for revenge considers her/his act justified. The murder is committed to "even the score," or to uphold the honor of the dead person and his/her family or community. In this case, the murderer is actually proud of the act and eager to take credit for it.

The problem with murder for revenge is that the story goes on. One murder leads to another in a chain that can only be broken when the responsibility for administering justice is yielded to a higher power, or when everyone is dead. In what we call civilisation, only the representative of the state acting on the outcome of a careful legal process can rightfully take a person's life. Of course, that process can be corrupted or simply mistaken, which is why folks like me are glad to live in a nation where the death penalty has been suspended. Ultimately, giving to a human institution the power deliberately to kill a human being can only be justified if we regard that institution as having the authority of God, the giver of life. The commandment against murder does not mean that murderers should not face justice. It means that the One who sets us free is also the One who will finally hold us accountable for how we live out our freedom, including how we respond to injustice. That freedom includes our ability to break free from the bondage of violence and injustice by refusing the path of revenge.

Another reason why people commit murder is fear. We imagine that someone is trying to hurt or kill us or someone we love, and so we kill them first. Those who commit such murder will seek to justify the murder as self-defense, and so not really murder. "I had to do it before he (or she) could do it to me." The problem with this excuse is obvious. When we use it, we claim to be God, knowing the heart, mind and intentions of another, having therefore the right to take away their life for a wrong they had not yet committed.

Fear, like anger, is a natural human emotion, not wrong in itself. Fear mobilizes our energy to perceive and respond to danger. It helps us be alert. So why is it that in the Bible one of the messages most frequently coming to humans from God or an angel is, "Be not afraid"? Well, I suppose meeting an angel or hearing the voice of God would make me afraid. But the problem of fear alone is that it can freeze us. The energy it generates can turn against us, taking away our power to confront the danger we perceive. So the point of the biblical "Be not afraid" must be: "I'm not here to overawe you; I'm here to move you!"

Fear needs a companion to produce movement. We may call that companion "courage." Fear accompanied by courage means you can face the fear and whatever is causing it. You can be moved to do what needs to be done in that scary situation, no matter how grim the prospect. So now imagine we are in a situation where our lives and the lives of our companions seem to be threatened by some nasty-looking people carrying weapons. Fear alone can freeze us. If we have courage, we will act. But how? Flight? Fight?

This is where the commandment and the freedom it offers make a difference. The Israelites lived in fear in Egypt. After all, the king tried to kill all their baby boys. With Moses' leadership, they found the courage to move, to attempt to leave Egypt for the desert. But the courage they found was a special kind, and it came to them as a gift. It was courage blended with the faith that the God of their ancestors was journeying with them. This kind of courage we may call "hope." Being able to face the scary stuff in life is good, but hope is even better. The Israelites could not see where they were going. It was trusting God's promise that changed their courage into hope, and that hope gave them a sense of possibility not limited to fight or flight. They no longer had to accept the definition of reality given to them in their life as slaves. Moved by hope, they saw the possibility of freedom and began the journey toward freedom in a promised land.

Now let's look again at our imagined life-threatening situation. We are rightly afraid. We have courage, and are prepared to do whatever we can to meet the danger. Our choice of actions is limited to our sense of the situation. If we assume that those others are heartless killers and that our only options are fight or flight, we may well accept murder as what we must do. But what if our courage is transformed into hope by our awareness of God's presence in our situation? What if hope—trust in God's promises— leads us to see the others as also God's beloved creatures? The commandment sets us free from bondage to fear, opening us to move in a way not determined by the way the situation initially appears.

Let's not imagine that the situation will magically turn out just fine, with no one hurt. That's not the way the biblical story runs, and that's not what God promises. But hope opens us to the freedom of new possibilities, the freedom of knowing that the situation does not determine the story, and the story is not over. Such is the dangerous and hopeful freedom toward which the commandment steers us.

The last five commandments are all tersely negative in form. "No murder" appears very simple. But the heart of murder can be expressed in more complicated ways. I can murder someone by provoking someone else to do it, by manipulating their capacity for anger or fear, or their need to be seen as an agent of "justice." I can become responsible for murder by providing aid, such as giving or selling a weapon, to someone I know or should reasonably suspect to have murderous intentions. I can murder someone by consenting to their murder, by keeping silent when I should be protesting against murderous acts. Or we can murder someone by merely withholding from them the necessities of life. We might even say that murder is committed when one person treats another in a way that is soul-destroying, such as encouraging a person to begin a behavior that is potentially addictive. (Thanks to St. Thomas Aquinas for helping me see these dimensions.)

Further, all these forms of murder can be political as well as personal. Living in a democracy, we all share responsibility for what happens when our nation sends troops into war, or permits the irresponsible sale of weapons, or fails to protect persecuted minorities, or becomes indifferent to the needs of the poor and homeless, or treats addicts as criminals rather than as people who need help. Once again we see that true freedom is a gift that can only be received when it is shared. Freedom belongs to life in community, not just to individuals.

We do not spell out these complications to the commandment to make it appear more difficult, but to show how following this path, despite the wholly negative form of these last five commandments, leads to action. Freedom involves moving forward, not just avoiding certain acts. No one has seen this more clearly than Martin Luther. In his *Small Catechism* he says this about the meaning of the Sixth Commandment: "*We are to fear and love God so that we do not hurt our neighbor in any way, but help him in all his physical needs.*" Living in a community where we help one another lifts the shadows of fear and rage, opening the way toward a climate of freedom in which we can help each other overcome the anger that blinds us, the self-idolatry of revenge, and the paralysis and panic fear produces when we think we are alone. We are never alone when we trust the promises of the One who calls us to walk together the path toward freedom.

10

The Seventh Commandment:
freedom for intimacy

You shall not commit adultery.

EXODUS 20:14

YOU MAY HAVE NOTICED that we have stopped quoting the Deuteronomy version. That is because, from here on, Deuteronomy differs from the Exodus version only by beginning each sentence, "Neither shall you. . ."

So here we are at adultery. Some cynic has suggested that adultery is what you do when you become an adult. While we do live in a time and culture in which this statement has become plausible, I will be arguing that this plausibility is more a judgment upon our culture than a revelation of a long-suppressed truth. I hope you, the reader, will consider the possibility that sexual intercourse apart from genuine intimacy between the people involved is in fact dehumanizing, a sign that freedom has been lost.

Of course, this means that we will have to think about what common usage refers to as "sex," even though this usage is far from the basic and simple meaning of the word. Think about it. "Are you having sex?" Well, how could I not? I am a member of a species in which sexual difference is crucial to reproduction. Every human has (a) sex although, as we have been discovering lately, assigning each person to a particular culturally-given sexual identity can, in some cases, be arbitrary to the point of confusion and cruelty. Let's agree not to press the question, "Which sex are you?" when the answer may be neither clear nor helpful. Sex, then, is something we "have" just by being human. What we do with it is the matter to which the Seventh Commandment speaks. As with the other commandments, it speaks a word, a promise, of freedom.

The order of the Commandments suggests that integrity in our sexual relations is a very important dimension of loving our neighbor, right after respecting life itself. However, that is not a good excuse for the sexual obsessions of some Christians and their churches over the centuries. Consider the following assertions: "Real Christians, especially Christian women, will be virginal, abstaining from sexual relations altogether." "Women cannot possibly be priests (or ministers)." "Priests must be celibate." "Sex is one of those topics about which Christians must never speak—except to pass judgment on the impure." "Anyone who loves and is sexually intimate with another person of the same sex is sinful and perverse, and must be excluded from the church." "Anyone whose sense of their sexual identity does not fit readily into the categories recognized by our culture is morally disordered."

These and similar convictions have been held by a majority of Christians at one time or another. It is easy to say that such statements are wrong, even inhumane. A Roman Catholic friend once made the point by saying the church had taught him that sex is dirty, and you should only do it with someone you love. It is less easy to show how the obsessiveness behind these so-called "Christian values" actually aggravates sexual disorder in the cultures where they are made, although the testimony of the victims of sexual abuse by church authorities should be sufficient evidence.

Strange as it may seem, I am proposing that we can use the bad example of typical Christian attitudes towards sexual intimacy to guide us to the true meaning of the commandment. What is important for our purpose is to locate the source of the obsession and to show how it restricts the freedom toward which the commandment points us. In taking this path, I certainly am not claiming to be above or better than other Christians. I have committed adultery. I am a recovering homophobe. My own quest for intimacy through sexual relations will never serve as a model for anyone, except perhaps for my persistence in the face of failure. What I offer here is such wisdom as I may have gained through my own sin and failure, and through the miracle of the Good News of forgiveness and redemption. I could have said the same thing about my reflections on all the other commandments but, for the sake of those who know me, it seems most important to do it here.

Why is sexual attraction so powerful? Too often Christians, contrary to the witness of their own scriptures, have taken it to be diabolical, one of those temptations from which we pray to be delivered. But what if it is powerful because God made it that way? Or, if we are taking the Third Commandment seriously, what if it is powerful because the evolutionary process has made it that way for most of us? Sexual attraction between human beings is one of the clearest signs that we are meant for life together, for life in community. So why the fear and loathing on the part of some folks who claim to be religious?

Maybe the "fear" part is not entirely wrong. There is a deeper sense of the word "fear." The Psalmist says that "*we are fearfully and wonderfully made.*" The Teacher of Wisdom tells us that "*the fear of the Lord is the beginning of wisdom.*" In this sense, sexual intimacy is a fearful thing when we are fully aware of what is going on. The liturgy for marriage in the old Book of Common Prayer warns us that a sexual union is to be entered into "*reverently, discreetly, and in the fear of God.*"

What is it about sexual intimacy that is truly fearful? Just this: body, mind and spirit go together. There is no wall between them. When I give my body intimately to another, I implicitly give my whole self. As the Genesis 2:24 puts it, ". . . they become one flesh."

Sexual intimacy implies mutual love; and love, properly understood, is not a feeling which may or may not last. It is an ordering of my will in which I hold the well-being of another at the center of my own well-being. Put more poetically, to love is to give another my heart, clearly a dangerous undertaking. We call sexual intimacy "love-making"; and that is exactly what it is meant to be.

However, we live in a culture which both affirms this truth and simultaneously gives us messages that contradict it. Too often, sexual intimacy is portrayed as a game which we play for the pleasure it gives us, a game in which there are winners and losers, a game in which the powerful win and the weak are exploited, even displayed as trophies.

This false "playfulness" can be understood as a reaction to the obsessive fearfulness of some Christian practice and teaching, but the results are no less harmful. In contrast to both these attitudes, sexual intimacy as expressive of love is fearful in the true sense, because love is risky. Loving makes me utterly vulnerable to another, totally exposed to loss and disappointment, just as it opens me to real joy. In love, nothing is ever "under control," although the view of marriage promulgated by many religious groups makes it sound as if control is the whole point.

So, sexual attraction is this powerful, fearful impetus towards "love-making." We can become obsessed by it, but only if we are overcome by the wrong kind of fear, the kind that makes it impossible to love. No one who believes that the love of God for us is most fully revealed by a crucified Messiah will underestimate the fearfulness of love, nor will they forget that "perfect love casts out fear."

Now back to the commandment: "You shall not commit adultery." Adultery does not mean something adults do. A different meaning of adultery operates here, one we can see in the word "adulterate." One definition of that word reads: "adulterate: to debase or make impure by adding inferior, alien, or less desirable materials or elements." To adulterate sexual intimacy might mean something like the obsessive attitude of too many Christians, too overcome by fear to engage in genuine love-making. Or it might mean engaging in sexual relations for the sake of personal pleasure, but without love. Or it might mean what it usually means, engaging in sexual intimacy when one or both persons have already given their bodies, and have pretended to give their hearts, to another. In all these cases the fearfulness, the power, the joy and the love implicit in sexual intimacy are adulterated.

Sexual attraction is a gift meant to lead us to love, and love has always been both the source and the goal of freedom. Do not be obsessed by the fear or blind to the possibility of love. Genuine sexual intimacy is beautiful and awesome as well as fearful. Do not adulterate it. Allow it to lead us toward the freedom of fearful, out-of-control, beautiful loving.

11

The Eighth Commandment: freedom for ownership

You shall not steal.

ON THE SURFACE, THIS commandment seems pretty simple. Do not take something that belongs to someone else. Why not? Well, we do not want someone else to take something that belongs to us. So if we all play by this rule, everyone will be safe, including us. By this reading, in which we take ownership as obvious, defined by current possession and legal precedent, I have never broken this commandment, making it the only one about which I can make that claim. Unfortunately for my claim, it is not so simple.

Let's start on the personal level. Sometimes stealing takes place in the open, using violence. We usually do not have trouble seeing that as wrong. Then there is theft, or sneaky stealing, like shoplifting. It appears that many of us find it easy to excuse that when we do it, and may even admire others who do it skillfully. And what about the time I found a $20 bill in a parking lot? Did I make any effort to find the person who might have lost it? Or suppose I want to unload some of my stuff and someone, perhaps out of ignorance or desperation, offers me much more than what I know it to be worth. Do I take what is offered, or only what I know to be a fair price? Or suppose I take a job, and discover that the supervision is lax. Is it stealing to give less than my full attention to the work, or to take some extra time off, and still be fully paid? The commandment might seem simple, but it is remarkably easy to excuse myself for taking advantage of opportunities to appropriate what I know belongs to another. In fact it is not hard to find people who will tell us that such sneaky stealing is actually a sign of ambition, an indication of our eagerness to "get ahead" in the world.

It gets even more complicated when we consider the social, political and economic dimensions of life. Sometimes it is fairly obvious. A bankruptcy law is passed which says that investors in a failed enterprise get their money back, but the pensioners who are owed their pensions as deferred wages get only what is left after everything else is settled. Legislators who have come to depend upon the contributions of the wealthy design tax systems which allow the wealthy to shelter their money from taxation while the rest of the population makes up the difference. Wealth allows some to buy promotion, power and recognition to which they would not otherwise be entitled. All these are forms of theft.

Less obvious is the robbery—stealing through violence—committed by governments, who sometimes call it war and sometimes colonization. North Americans are increasingly becoming aware of the fact that most of us are able to call our nation "ours" only because the land was taken, sometimes by violence and sometimes by intimidation or deceit, from those who were here before. This colonial expansion by European nations, which allowed them to exploit the natural resources of Africa, Asia and the Americas, was the basis for the emergence of the economic system we call Capitalism, a system in which those who have wealth can use it to make more. While some nations have found ways to mitigate partially some of the problems this system inevitably produces, the logic of a purely capitalist economy leads to ever increasing inequality and environmental degradation. When people submit to this outcome and regard it as somehow just, we may call it sneaky stealing—theft. When this system is upheld by violence and political corruption, we may call it robbery. Either way, those of us who benefit from a capitalist economy (for example, those who, as I do, profit from retirement funds) are complicit in the violation of this commandment. Even if it is perfectly legal and admired as a sign of success, and even if we are unaware of those from whom our wealth is taken, we are violating the commandment: "No stealing." I am well aware of the argument that Capitalism, by fostering economic growth, serves the common good by making us all, eventually, richer. But as long as economic growth is distributed unequally and the human future threatened by unsustainable exploitation of natural resources, I remain convinced that the commandment is warning us that our freedom is being lost.

Since it appears to be impossible to avoid stealing while living in this present world, how can the commandment lead to freedom rather than to condemnation, especially since recent experience seems to indicate that an anti-capitalist revolution leads to alternatives which turn out to be even more restrictive of freedom? I believe there is a way of looking at and living out ownership which is non-violently subversive of Capitalism in its current form, and which expresses economically the freedom to which God calls us.

"Do not steal" is a clear affirmation of ownership, except that we begin by recognizing the ownership of others and reasoning from there to ourselves, rather than beginning in the self-interested way we noted above (If I want to protect mine, I should let others protect theirs). This affirmation of ownership through a commandment given to the community called Israel opens our eyes to recognize that not only our freedom but everything we have to sustain our lives is a gift. The Israelites were slaves in Egypt. They did not *have* property; they *were* property. God brought them into the wilderness and gave them such food (manna) and water (from a rock) as were needed. Eventually they were led to a land where they could prosper, a land of "milk and honey." Property and goods are given to us to sustain our life in community. The reason not to take the goods or property of our neighbor is because God has given life-sustaining ownership to the neighbor, and to us. What we own is given to us for a good purpose by the One who loves us and has set us on freedom road.

The commandment, then, calls us to recognize the gift and purpose of ownership. It calls us to gratitude and responsibility. Christians have sometimes spoken of this as exercising stewardship. A free community is one in which each person recognizes what has been given to them. That is why we do not steal, and that is how we experience the freedom of ownership for ourselves. Martin Luther put it very well in his *Brief Catechism*: "*We are to fear and love God so that we do not take our neighbor's money or property, or get them in any dishonest way, but help* [the neighbor] *to improve and protect his* [or her] *property and means of making a living.*"

How is this subversive of what we call Capitalism? Let's start on the personal and local level. Focusing first on the needs and rights of our neighbor rather than our own, the commandment gives us a different perspective on our economic activity. For example, I may have a job. Its first purpose is helping those I am working for and with to serve the community in a particular way. Let's say I wait on tables in a restaurant. The purpose of the establishment is to serve tasty, nutritious and healthy food to its customers at a reasonable price. Fulfilling this purpose makes the community a better place. My purpose is to help the customers feel welcome, help them choose a good meal, bring them their food in a prompt and friendly way, and perhaps clear the table when they are finished, thus helping them have the most enjoyable, healthy experience possible. Fulfilling that purpose serves both my customers and my employer.

When I see my work in that way, it is no longer just a job. It has become a vocation. I own the work as my expression of who I am and of how I am able to serve my community. Consequently, I own the fruits of my work, and I am responsible for judging how best to use them in the enjoyment of life and the service of my family, friends and community. My work becomes an expression of my freedom in a free community.

But wait! Isn't the purpose of a business to make as much profit as possible? Isn't the purpose of a job to make as much money as possible? I promised you a way to be subversive. Now you can begin to see what I mean. An economic system whose goal is merely to enrich my business, my shareholders, and my bank account as much as possible is clearly destructive of community, its quality of life and, finally, its freedom. Since I am part of that community, my freedom is finally compromised as well. Anyone who goes to work out of necessity alone is, in truth, a slave. Those who hire others only in order to advance their own interests are, in a sense, slave owners.

We have moved from the personal dimension through the economic and social dimensions. Now we may move to the political. I am arguing that the commandment against stealing has powerful political implications. Domestically, it means that the purpose of government is to serve the common good.

Public policy and law should respect and encourage responsible ownership, but not just for some, such as wealthy potential contributors to election campaigns. Public education, health care, housing policy and environmental, labor and taxation laws have a vital role to play in encouraging all citizens to engage in ownership, that is, to live their lives in a way which enables them to make a contribution to their community. To doctrinaire socialists, this probably sounds conservative. To doctrinaire conservatives, this probably sounds socialist. Can you see why I regard it as non-coercively subversive of Capitalism? In our current political and social climate, the common good is taken to mean the sum of private goods. But if we understand the freedom of ownership in the context of the commandments, we see that faithful ownership means responsibility to and for our community. For example, that means owning our natural environment in such a way that this precious and amazing gift of God is not being stolen from future generations.

Finally, let us ask a few questions about how freedom of ownership might influence relations between nations and their governments. Is the current obsession with the security of boundaries, expressed in its most extreme form by the building of walls, an expression of freedom or of fear? Is military engagement in the internal conflicts of other nations a way to help protect the freedom of our neighbors, or is it done to protect our own economic interests in the region? Can empire-building, including the economic empires of Capitalism, result in true commonwealth, or is it always a form of domination and theft? When we take seriously the commandment against stealing, it will influence the ways we understand and answer such questions.

12

The Ninth Commandment: freedom for friendship

You shall not bear false witness against your neighbor.

Exodus 20:16

JUST AT THE POINT where we might expect a commandment prohibiting the telling of lies, we get something different but related. Instead of commanding us always to tell the truth, the focus is on what is good for our neighbor. Who can rightly claim to know the whole truth anyway? Perhaps the absence of such a commandment is a way of recognizing that any human who makes such a claim has cast him/herself in the role of God, and is already breaking the First Commandment.

I am not arguing for relativism. Creation has become the way it is, and not the way we would imagine or desire it to be. There is such a thing as truth, and it stands in implicit judgment on all our claims to know it. If there is no truth, that would apply also to the claim that there is no truth. The fact that we deliberately communicate with one another presumes the existence of truth. Otherwise this is just gibberish, marks on a page. That we are creatures of language testifies to truth, and our attempts at communication imply our obligation to seek truth even as we sense that it can never be fully in our possession.

Further, communication implies that our search toward truth involves community. Everything we say to each other, no matter how trivial or conventional, carries with it a usually unspoken and often unintended implication: "This is the truth *as I see and understand it, and as well as I can express it*." As we speak, we implicitly offer this to our neighbor and expect some response, one that will by opposition or correction or affirmation lead us closer to truth and to the neighbor. So it makes sense for this commandment to focus directly on how our speaking affects our neighbor and our life in community.

"You shall not bear false witness against your neighbor." Gender-exclusive language aside, Martin Luther's *Small Catechism* goes to the radical heart of this Commandment. "*We are to fear and love God so that we do not betray, slander, or lie about our neighbor, but defend, speak well of, and explain his actions in the kindest way.*" The evil of slander and lies is obvious, for it means saying things we know not to be true. As for "do not betray," I take betrayal to mean revealing the weaknesses, mistakes and vulnerability we have observed in our neighbor to those who have no need to know such things, and who might exploit such knowledge to harm the neighbor. Gossip is one form of betrayal, one which tempts us as an opportunity to appear superior to those we betray.

When Luther turns to the positive implications of the commandment, the insights are breath-taking. To defend and speak well of my neighbor does not mean countering gossip with contrary lies. If I know my neighbor has done something wrong, it does not help for me to deny it when I hear it spoken of. What helps is to insist that she is still my neighbor, and that her actions need to be understood in their full context. When, in John's Gospel, Jesus is confronted with a mob accusing a woman of adultery and preparing for her execution, he does not deny her sin. Rather, he puts it in context. "Let anyone who is without sin among you cast the first stone." When the execution has thus been halted, he offers the woman forgiveness and a fresh start. The point of noticing our neighbors' shortcomings is to help them find a better path without self-righteous condemnation. The commandment to not bear false witness is a call to be free from the judgmental self-righteousness that builds barriers between us. It is an invitation to reach out in honest friendship.

Our ability to be a friend grows as we come to understand our neighbor better. The more deeply we know our neighbor, the more fully we can put his actions into a truthful context. Only as we come to know the struggles, sorrows and wounds of our neighbor can we explain her actions "in the kindest way." The path toward which we are pointed by the Ninth Commandment is one in which the negative things we see in the lives of those around us become invitations to know those folks better, to help them and allow them to help us become better, and so to strengthen the community. This can be a community as small as a family or a neighborhood, and as large as our imagination can reach. The freedom it offers is a freedom we can only know through opening ourselves to friendship.

When I say "help them . . . become better," I have a specific experience in mind. I was privileged to do my doctoral studies in the Divinity School of the University of Chicago. This included some seminars, small classes involving students near the completion of their studies. You might expect these to be highly competitive, with each person aiming to prove themselves best qualified for the limited number of teaching and research positions available to graduates, and highly critical of the work of others. You would be right to expect this, but what I experienced in those seminars changed my understanding of what true competition can be. Each of us took the projects and proposals of the other students as if they were our own. We tore each other's work to shreds, not to destroy it, but to show how it could be done better. Each of us came away with much better work than we could have done on our own. Each of us was teacher to the other, willing to give our full attention and insight to the other's proposal. These seminars became super-charged competitions to see who could be most helpful to the other scholars. Friendship as correction, understood from this model, is not "being nice," overlooking the faults of our friends and neighbors, but taking the risk of offering all we have in helping them be the persons they truly want to be. There is a freedom in this kind of friendship that is far from the constraints of niceness and conformity. But it requires us to be fully open to the others, to understand them as fully as possible, so that we can ". . . explain his actions in the kindest way." It also requires us to be open to correction by our neighbors, to appreciate it as encouragement for growth.

Unfortunately, there is a strong current in our culture teaching us that freedom and success is a zero-sum game, that in order for me to win, everyone else has to lose. We see this too often in our sports. Trash-talking is admired and sportsmanship is sometimes seen as a lack of competitive spirit. I do not believe this current can prevail, but it will only be corrected when we are willing and able to understand why so many are caught up in it, and what life experiences have led them down this path.

This commandment also has a political dimension. Our civilization is justly proud of its democratic politics. Democracy allows each one of us to be involved in governing as well as being governed. Our political community is open to the exercise of citizenship by all, and that is surely something to be celebrated. However, the form of our political process, the structures through which our democracies normally operate, and the expectations of our political culture contain elements which make observance of the Ninth Commandment difficult. Once again, the commandment is subversive of our cultural norms, and calls into question our pretension to be part of a "Free World."

Consider the fact that both our judicial system and our electoral and legislative processes are adversarial. We expect our judges and our juries to be fair and impartial; that part is good. But we also expect the evidence on the basis of which they must judge to be presented in the most one-sided way possible. The prosecution is expected to present the defendant in the worst possible way, while the defense is expected to impugn the character and reliability of the prosecution witnesses as completely as possible. Our attorneys make their reputations on their ability to do these things; were they to be seen to be following the Ninth Commandment, it might open them to the charge of malpractice.

In our Capitalist economy, the common good is expected to emerge from maximizing selfish behavior. In our judicial system, justice is expected to result from maximizing a biased presentation of the facts. In both cases, freedom is seen as something pertaining to the participants only as individuals. Since economic and social inequality means that some people can afford "better" representation than others, it is not surprising that cynicism about the justice system should be expressed by many.

When we look at our partisan political process, the problem is perhaps even more obvious. It is not unreasonable to expect that, in our political communities, different and sometimes directly conflicting perspectives should be found. Our differing experiences naturally lead us to imagine the common good differently. In fact, the existence and expression of these differences often makes us a better and stronger community. That these differences should find expression through political organizations—parties—is neither surprising nor wrong. The problems arise from the interaction of the representatives of these parties with one another and with the electorate. When electoral success, winning elections and holding power, becomes the only or even the primary criterion of political success, both the Ninth Commandment and the common good become at best irrelevant. Freedom is for winners only, and is identical with power. To the extent that this is a fair description of our political climate, the skepticism and political indifference of a large part of the population is easy to understand, and the freedom of our political community is put at risk.

How might the Ninth Commandment help us imagine and move toward a democratic politics in which the common good, not the success of my party, is the criterion of success? I believe that the refusal to bear false witness against my political neighbor, the exercise of the freedom to explain the actions (policies, votes, etc.) of my political neighbor "in the kindest possible way," would lead to the revitalization of the political climate and the enhancement of freedom in our public life. A climate of mutual respect is far freer than an atmosphere of distrust and animosity.

Again, we should not imagine that politics will ever be about "niceness." Debate about matters of justice in our broken world will always call for passion and commitment to the cause. It would be foolish to expect easy consensus in a world of irreducible diversity. But the Ninth Commandment guides us toward respect for the humanity of all our neighbors, even those with political views which seem to us seriously misguided. The freedom offered by a climate of respect would, at the very least, discourage those who seek elective office solely as a way of enhancing their own personal power and reputation, and would encourage others to submit themselves to the risks of electoral politics as a way of contributing to the common good.

Finally, it seems reasonable to hope that such a change in climate would lead many of those who have become cynical non-voters to take on the tasks of participating in discussion and debate, making up their own minds, and exercising the rights of citizenship. Would that not make us all freer?

13

The Tenth Commandment: the freedom of gratitude

You shall not covet your neighbor's house; you shall not covet your neighbor's wife, or male or female slave, or ox, or donkey, or anything that belongs to your neighbor.

EXODUS 20:17

UP TO THIS POINT, the commandments seem directed towards our actions, telling us what to do (honor your parents, observe the day of rest) or not do (no killing, no stealing, etc.). Now, at the end, we have one directed toward our thoughts and desires. Is this not asking too much of us? Who can perfectly control their thoughts and desires?

Besides, is it not seeing what is good in the lives of our friends and neighbors that rightly shapes our own desires and efforts? This commandment seems to attack my will to succeed in life at its very source. What difference does it make if I covet my neighbor's donkey, or Chevy, or collection of beer mugs, as long as I do not do anything about it? This is, for sure, a hard commandment to keep. I have broken it all too often. But it is not unreasonable or life-denying. Like the other commandments, it is an important step on the path toward freedom. Let's look at it more closely.

To covet means to desire to take for ourselves something that belongs to another. But what if something good in the life of a near or distant neighbor awakens in me the desire to have the same thing, or something like it but even better? My neighbor has a beautiful garden. What harm is there in wanting to have an even more beautiful garden? My classmate gets really good marks. Why should I not desire to get better ones? The answer depends upon how and why I intend to fulfill my desire. If I intend to compete with my neighbor in a way that harms his garden or impedes her academic prowess, the previous commandments already warn me off. If I desire what I see as good in my neighbor's life so that I can feel superior to him, then we can say that I am coveting.

If my awakened desire is good for both me and my neighbor, then we can rejoice in the healthy competition which results. Young children covet naturally as part of developing a sense of self. But as we mature, we realize that life is "not just about me." Our capacity for desire is the natural basis of our ability to love. When we covet, our desires turn in upon ourselves, reverting to spiritual infancy. The Tenth Commandment is a call to grow up, to shape our desires in the direction of freedom for love and community.

The commandment gives us a list of objects which we are not to covet. Why the list, and why the order of the items? Surely my neighbor's wife is more important to him than his house, people more than property! The version in Deuteronomy 5:21 seems to think so, for it lists "wife" first and in a separate sentence. But there is a simplicity and clarity to the Exodus version of this commandment which we can see if we remember that the term "house" (*bet* in Hebrew) can mean something much more than but inclusive of the building in which the neighbor lives. In that way, it is rather like our word "church." In the narrow and common sense, a church is a building. When we say that someone "goes to church," we mean that they show up at a particular building at a designated time, but we know that the expression means more than that. The designated time is a time when a community gathers to worship. In its broader and deeper sense, "church" means a community of people sharing a faith and the journey involved with that faith; and "going to church" means taking one's place in that community.

In the same way, "house," in its broader and deeper sense, means the totality of someone's life-situation. The word is sometimes used to describe a commercial empire or an extended family. When we say that someone has lost "house and home," we are saying that the whole framework of their life has been lost. So the commandment lists the parts of "house" in proper order: life partner & family, job, possessions. To covet is to want all or part of a neighbor's life in a way that diminishes the neighbor.

A clear example of coveting is found in II Samuel 11 and 12. King David sees a beautiful woman, Bathsheba, bathing on her rooftop. He desires her to the point of arranging for the death of her husband, one of David's bravest military leaders. David's coveting of Bathsheba leads down the path to their son Solomon, David's successor; it also leads eventually to domestic violence, civil war, and the division of the kingdom. Coveting by the leader chosen by God leads toward a loss of freedom by all the people, a path that ends in the destruction of Solomon's Temple and exile. The commandment is not some private, personal matter; it has massive social and political implications.

As we said above, desire is the natural basis of love. To love someone or something is to focus our desire upon her or him or it. To covet is to focus my desire upon myself. But the commandments, as we have seen, can be summarized as the call to love God, the giver of life and freedom, and to love your neighbor as yourself. So this commandment is not some effort at thought control, the ultimate restriction at the end of a list of prohibitions. Rather, it leads us back to the beginning of the commandments and shows how they are unified. Far from restricting desire, the commandments ground our desire in its source, the gift of life itself, and lead it to maturity. We are not called to suppress desire, but to open ourselves to its breadth and depth. I am not asked to

83

stop loving myself, but to love the neighbor as I love myself. To covet is to turn my back on the source of my freedom, and to open the door to the false god More and its companions. To turn away from the immaturity of coveting is to find the thread which holds all the commandments together.

Consider the kind of freedom toward which this commandment leads us. I am neighbor to someone with a better "house" and an apparently finer quality of life than I seem to have. I can feel miserable coveting that house and what goes on in it. What is the alternative, the way in which I can walk joyfully? I could be grateful that my neighbors have been given such a gift. I could, to put it another way, be happy for them. Let's use another example. I am hoping to be promoted in my place of work, but the latest promotion goes to a colleague. I can covet that promotion, nurture resentment against that colleague, and draw away; or I can rejoice with her and, through that, perhaps come to know that person better. In the process, I may come to realize that the cost of that promotion was too high. My colleague has given away too much of the rest of life in the process of winning the promotion, and now needs my support and friendship. Or I may come to realize that my colleague really deserved that promotion, and that the move has made my workplace better, and better for me as well.

In each case, the alternative to coveting is the path of gratitude. When we look on the world around us, our first and deepest response can be gratitude for the gifts we have been and are being given, including the gift of life itself. In the prayer that Jesus taught his disciples, we pray: "Give us this day our daily bread." Not too much (More), and not too little. To pray those words in faith means to trust that our prayer will be and is being answered, that we have and will have enough. It is that kind of trust that frees us for gratitude and joy.

Of course, this does not mean that the world is all as it should be. We are not to be blind to the needs of those around us, or imagine that we should just sit there and take whatever comes along. Injustice and evil are part of our world, and they are to be resisted. Among the gifts we are given is the gift of having the energy, imagination, resources and community support sufficient to seek justice and resist evil in the world around us. That is one of the gifts for which we can be most grateful. Yes, we are called to work for the good of our community. But if that work arises from resentment, moralizing, and being judgmental, it will be not only ineffectual, we will be miserable while doing it. We are called to be joyful warriors for justice and peace, and that joy comes from gratitude for the gifts we have been given and will be given. Such warriors will never be victims, and will always be free, no matter how long and hard the struggle.

14

The Christ and the Commandments

WE NOTED EARLY ON that while the faith of Sarah and Abraham is shared by Jews, Muslims and Christians, the story is told differently by each, therefore the interpretation of the Commandments will be different in each tradition and within various versions of the traditions. I have written this as a Christian, and therefore must now give an account of how I understand the way it makes my interpretation different, not only that of from Jews and Muslims, but also from the interpretation of some other Christians. For example, Jews see the Ten Commandments as among the 613 Commandments found in our shared scripture. Yes, the ten have a special place in that context, but a Jew (my cousin Susan, for example) would remind me of the third set of ten, the one found in Exodus 34. This new set of ten is quite different from the two we have been examining.

I am not qualified to debate the interpretation of the Commandments with Jewish scholars. I am glad that Jewish and Christian scholars do just that among themselves and with each other, and I expect we will continue to be enriched by what comes from those discussions. But I did claim, early in this writing, that Jesus agrees with the Law given through Moses, and that the Ten Commandments are at the heart of his teaching. Now, in finishing, I must attempt to make good on that claim by giving a fuller account. How do I, as someone trying to live out the faith of the Christian community, see the place of the commandments in the New Testament witness to the life, death and resurrection of Jesus?

First of all, what do we know about Jesus, and how do we know it? We have the four stories of Jesus' life called "gospels" (meaning "good news") found in the New Testament. There are many more such stories, but the councils of the early church decided that these four were the official ones. Of course, people are still composing stories about Jesus, sometimes making them into musicals or films. While I appreciate all such efforts, as each bears its own truth, I will stick to the official four as my sources in this writing. In fact, each one of the four official stories carries its own truth, its unique contribution to shaping our encounter with the Christ. There are also many and diverse voices in the rest of the New Testament, the part made up of letters. It seems the councils of the church which made the decisions about what to include were determined to emphasize that no single version of the story and its message would ever be enough.

So what do Jesus' words, actions and being, as witnessed to by the New Testament, add to our understanding of the commandments? The Gospels record many times when Jesus got into arguments with the religious authorities over the commandments and their meaning. For example, early in Mark's Gospel (2:23–3:6) there is a controversy over the sabbath commandment. Jesus' disciples "pluck heads of grain" while walking. They are then accused of breaking the sabbath, presumably because the plucking is regarded as a form of labor. Mark clearly wants the accusation to look as frivolous as possible. Jesus responds by citing the example of David taking sacred bread from the "house of God" to feed himself and his hungry companions, shifting the issue. *"The sabbath was made for humankind, and not humankind for the sabbath,"* Jesus declares. The scene then shifts to a synagogue, where there is a man with "a withered hand." His opponents are watching for more sabbath violations, and Jesus challenges them. "Is it lawful to do good on the sabbath, to save life or to kill?," he asks. When the accusers are silent, Jesus heals the hand; and the accusers "immediately" (Mark's favorite word) begin to conspire with others "to destroy him." Mark thus connects Jesus' teaching about the sabbath, by word and deed, with the cause of his crucifixion. His teaching, it seems to me, is that the commandment is meant to liberate us for meeting human needs rather than restricting the scope of human action on a particular day of the week.

In another story that appears with interesting variations in three gospels (Mark 10, Luke 18 and Matthew 19), a man asks Jesus what he needs to do "to inherit eternal life." In Mark's story, Jesus' answer is terse. "You know the commandments. . ." Jesus then names some of the ten: no murder, adultery, theft, or false witness; honor parents. He also includes one which has puzzled commentators: "You shall not defraud." It seems related to what comes next. The man claims to have "kept all these since my youth." Jesus challenges the man to take one more step, to sell all his possessions, give the money to the poor, and become a follower of Jesus. "*When he heard this, he was shocked and went away grieving, for he had many possessions.*" Keeping the commandments is good, but the point of doing so is not to enhance one's status in this world or the next, but to walk the path of freedom. The man in this story is a slave to his wealth and status. Perhaps Jesus is elaborating on the Tenth Commandment in these words.

The gospel of Matthew, more than the other three, portrays Jesus as a teacher of the Law, a true successor to Moses. Early in the story (chapters 5-7) Jesus, having drawn a crowd, goes "up the mountain" to deliver his teaching. After giving the eight blessings called "the Beatitudes," and calling on us to let our light shine so that others will see our good works and give glory to our "Father in heaven," we encounter these words: "*Do not think that I have come to abolish the law or the prophets; I have come not to abolish but to fulfill.*" Jesus goes on to elaborate on that fulfillment. Do not murder? Yes, but also do not be angry with or insult "your brother or sister." And if you break this commandment, do not seek forgiveness from God before becoming reconciled with your neighbor. Do not commit adultery? Yes, but also do not look upon someone with lust, because what is in your heart matters as much as what you do. Love your neighbor? Yes, but also love your enemies and pray for those who persecute you.

This radicalization of the commandments is the core of Jesus' teaching, in these chapters and elsewhere. Chapter Six of the Sermon on the Mount can be read as a radicalization of the commandment against idolatry, including the idolatries of religion and wealth. The good news according to Matthew includes taking the commandments to a deeper level, not leaving them behind.

The metaphor of the "house" which we encountered in the Tenth Commandment supplies the conclusion to this time of teaching on the mountain. A person who "hears these words and acts on them" is like one who builds a house on rock, but to hear them and not act on them is like building a house on sand. So Matthew's Jesus is the one who comes to restore and renew the power and promise of Israel's path toward freedom. This theme runs through Matthew's entire story. On keeping the sabbath? See 12:1–14. On adultery? See 19:3–9. On honoring your parents? See 15:1–20. Jesus' final words to his disciples in this gospel direct them to *"make disciples of all nations. . .teaching them to obey everything that I have commanded you. . ."* The path toward freedom is now, after the resurrection, open to everyone.

Luke, unlike Matthew, does not portray Jesus primarily as a teacher of the law, but rather as the one who comes to establish a new Israel. This is never clearer than in a story unique to Luke, the parable of the Good Samaritan (10:25–37). It begins with material Luke shares with Matthew and Mark, a question about which is the most important commandment. Here the questioner is "a lawyer," and the answer the lawyer gives is the one we have already seen: love God and love your neighbor as yourself. Jesus agrees, but the lawyer, "wanting to justify himself," asks: "And who is my neighbor?" This evokes Jesus' story of the man who, on the road from Jerusalem to Jericho, is robbed and left on the roadside "half dead." Two representatives of the religious aristocracy see him but "passed by on the other side." A Samaritan stops to help, and goes to considerable lengths to see to the man's welfare. The Samaritan is declared to be the one who fulfills the commandment. Jesus challenges the lawyer to "go and do likewise."

The ironic point is that the Samaritans are regarded as enemies by the people of Israel. Samaritans are not just seen as outsiders but as close neighbors who, despite sharing a past, deliberately reject Israelite practices and values. Luke is saying, here and elsewhere in his story, that it is such outsiders who will participate in the new Israel God is calling together. The two basic commandments are still important, but Jesus has come to expand radically the scope of the community who will live them. When the Risen Christ appears to his disciples for the last time, he reminds them: "Everything written about me in the law of Moses, the prophets, and the psalms must be fulfilled." This means, he goes on to tell them, that his death and resurrection is meant to offer repentance and the forgiveness of sins "to all nations," and that they are soon to be commissioned to deliver this message. Luke's sequel, *The Acts of the Apostles*, continues the story, and the rest of the New Testament illustrates it.

One of the last of Jesus' teachings in Mark's gospel is also shared with Matthew and Luke (Mark 12, Matthew 22, and Luke 10). Here there is no controversy. In the Temple in Jerusalem, a scholar asks Jesus which commandment is "the first of all." In answering, Jesus does not single out one of the Ten Commandments. Instead he summarizes the Ten by quoting passages (Deuteronomy 6:5 and Leviticus 19:18), two commandments rather than ten. Love God with all that you have, and love your neighbor as yourself. Both dimensions of the commandments, the vertical and the horizontal, are lifted up. Jesus' questioner agrees with him, adding that these are *much more important than all whole burnt offerings and sacrifices.* Notice that this is said in the Temple, where the offerings and sacrifices take place. Jesus replies, *You are not far from the kingdom of God.*

This move to simplify the commandments finds its strongest expression in John's gospel, and in the letters that bear his name. In chapter 13, Jesus is having a last meal with his disciples before his arrest, trial and execution. After washing the disciples' feet—showing that true leadership is service—and sending out the disciple who was going to betray him to the authorities, Jesus says to his followers: "*I give you a new commandment, that you love one another. Just as I have loved you, you also should love one another. By this everyone will know that you are my disciples, if you have love for one another.*" Near the end of this time together, in Chapter 15, with the crucifixion looming, Jesus returns to the theme. "*This is my commandment, that you love one another as I have loved you. No one has greater love than this, to lay down one's life for one's friends.*" The summary of the commandments, to love God and the neighbor, is about to be embodied as Jesus goes to the Cross; and Jesus' followers, now called his friends, are commanded to follow this example of the radical nature of love.

If we are tempted to see this condensation and embodiment of the commandments as setting aside what was given to the Israelites as their path to freedom, the letters of Paul provide a sure correction. Two letters in particular, to the Romans and to the Galatians, focus on the relationship between the original covenant with its commandments and the renewal of that covenant given as a gift to all of us in the life, death and resurrection of Jesus. Let us have a look at the letter to the Romans, if you will pardon my very simplified view of a work on which so many great teachers have poured their attention.

Evidently, the church in Rome had both Jewish and Gentile members. Paul has not yet been to Rome, but he knows many of the Christians there, and he knows there are problems. One of these is the relationship between those of Jewish and those of Gentile (that is, not Jewish) origins, and the letter is aimed at clarifying and healing this relationship. After beginning on a personal note, acknowledging that he has been called to preach the good news to the Gentiles, he goes directly into the subject of the letter. Here is the transition (1:16–17): " . . . *I am not ashamed of the gospel; it is the power of God for salvation to everyone who has faith*, to the Jew first [my emphasis] *and also to the Greek . . . as it is written*, [now he quotes one of the prophets of Israel] *the one who is righteous will live by faith.*" This sets the tone of the entire letter. The message, as far as I can understand it, is this:

Everyone is broken. The Gentiles could have known God's way from creation, but they turned away to idolatry. The Jews received the Law, but they have not followed it. Now Jesus, crucified and risen, as anticipated in the Law and by the prophets, has opened for all of us the path toward setting things right. *"So the law is holy, and the commandment is holy and just and good"* (7:12), but keeping the commandments is not something we can do on our own. Our brokenness turns the Law into a curse for us. We can, by trusting in what Jesus has done for us, live the freedom God promised through the commandments. We are still broken human beings, Jews and Gentiles alike; but now *"nothing will be able to separate us from the love of God in Christ Jesus our Lord."* (8:39). God has used the disobedience of Israel as a way to open the promise of freedom to all nations, but the Jews *"are beloved, for the sake of their ancestors; for the gifts and the calling of God are irrevocable."* (11:28–29)

The letter goes on to spell out for the Romans, in their particular circumstances, what the path toward freedom looks like. They are to use their individual gifts to serve each other and the community. As in the Gospels, the commandments are radicalized and the Old Testament is quoted in support.

> *"Owe no one anything, except to love one another; for the one who loves another has fullfilled the law. The commandments, "You shall not commit adultery; You shall not murder; You shall not steal; You shall not covet"; and any other commandment, are summed up in this word, 'Love your neighbor as yourself.' Love does no wrong to a neighbor; therefore, love is the fulfilling of the law."* (13:8–10)

Paul concludes by warning against the danger of self-righteousness and the temptation to be judgmental of others.

If I have understood this letter rightly, it is a good summary of the way the Ten Commandments remain central in the description of the path Jesus calls his followers to walk, even as the commandments are interpreted in a deep way, one that makes their orientation to freedom unmistakable.

15

Faith and Freedom:
a postscript

THE CAUTIOUS READER WILL rightly detect the presence of a circle in this writing. My formation as a particular kind of Christian, my way of reading the New Testament and especially Paul's letter to the Romans, my understanding of the Ten Commandments, my use of words such as "faith" and "freedom," my presentation of these thoughts to you in a way that suggests they might have a claim upon your life as well as mine: all these are parts of a circle. Each one depends upon the others. If at any point my account becomes deceptive, manipulative or self-serving, the whole enterprise becomes suspect.

Suspicion is most likely to arise when words are used in a way that subverts their normal meaning. Because I am aware that I have used at least two important words that way, I want to be clear about what they could and should mean for us, and about why I reject their usual meaning. This does not and cannot involve breaking the circle; my understanding of these words has been formed by my interpretation of the Bible and its story and vice versa. But since

I have presented this account as a story that makes a claim upon our lives, and since I warned at the beginning that I would be using these words differently, and since using key words subversively can lead one to be significantly and even dangerously alienated from the world as it is, I owe it to you, the reader, to be "up front" about my use of these words.

Let's start with "faith." Christians are at least partly responsible for the way faith has come to be (wrongly, in my opinion) understood. The reformation movements in Western Europe that peaked in the 16th Century used formal statements of faith, often called creeds or confessions, to define themselves, usually so they could claim recognition and support from ruling powers. In the rationalistic culture that, in the following centuries, arose out of disillusionment with conflicts justified by religious differences, theology came to be understood as the intellectual defense of these creeds and confessions. "Faith" came to be understood as an intellectual construct used to separate one group from another. Not surprisingly, "creed," with its connotations of division and intellectual rigidity, became a negative term, even for many Christians. "Faith" came to be synonymous with "belief," an arbitrary and non-rational intellectual constuct. As modern science became a dominant and trusted source of intellectual authority, faith-as-belief was seen by many as tolerable at best, a form of damage control in the face of unavoidable evils such as death, something the brave and realistic could do without.

In the story of Israel and its winding path toward freedom, faith has a very different meaning. "Faith" in the biblical context is the willingness to trust the call to walk that path. To have faith means to respond positively to the summons of the nameless God, I AM. It is not a belief, in the sense of an intellectual judgement. It is an orientation, finding a direction toward a destination given by a promise. The shape of that orientation is given in the Ten Commandments and their two-dimensional summary; love God and love your neighbor as yourself. So faith, in the biblical sense, means trusting in a promise.

One important contrast between this faith-as-trust and faith-as-belief is that biblical faith is about my relationship to others,

95

while faith-as-belief is just about me. Faith-as-belief might involve some rules to live by, but the point of living by them is to be a "good person." It is no surprise that faith-as-belief has led many people to think that the point of being a Christian is "to get to heaven when I die," even though that notion is thoroughly unbiblical. The biblical journey of faith is made as part of a community, including that widest possible community, the whole of creation. God's promise is that the power of death will be overcome, because death is what separates us from one another. It is a promise made to and for the world God has created, not a promise to transfer individuals to some imaginary world. To use the language of traditional theology, it is a promise of resurrection, not individual immortality.

So when we speak of faith in the context of the biblical story, "faith" means trust in the promises of the God of Israel and willingness to walk the path towards the fulfillment of those promises. We may call that path "freedom road" because it begins with liberation from slavery in "Egypt" and points toward liberation from the death-dealing power of the gods of empire, wherever they may be manifest.

As with "faith," "freedom" has come to have a very different meaning in the world-as-it-is. Here it may take an idealistic form, as in "You can be whatever you choose to be." Or it may appear in its more brutal form: "I can do whatever I please." In either case, it is a freedom which belongs to me as an individual, as a possession, while freedom in the biblical sense belongs to us as a community, as a gift. Just as the meaning of faith has been distorted by becoming individualized and subjective, so the meaning of freedom has been distorted by becoming individualized and possessive.

What evidence can I present to support the claim that this way of imagining freedom is distorted? I can only invite you to reflect upon the world of possessive individualism. What strikes me most about that world is the prevalence of fear, anxiety and loneliness.

In a zero-sum world where every profit for someone is a loss for someone else, we are always potential losers. We sense that what we have has been taken from others, and we fear their retribution. We arm ourselves psychologically and sometimes literally against those whose freedom we have taken, even as we reassure ourselves that the harm was not done by us as individuals, so we cannot be responsible. In the name of freedom, we live in fear.

In a consumer society of possessive individualism, we must live with the anxiety of never having enough. "Gotta' have that!" is the motto that betrays our claim to freedom as a hollow cover for conformism. Technological advance offers the promise that we will be free from the need to work, but that promise veils the threat that we will be unemployed, no longer needed by those who are admired for their ability to say, "You're fired." Our work is seen as a prison of anxiety, rather than an opportunity to serve our neighbors.

In a world where we gather in ever-increasing numbers and our cities are ranked by population rather than by quality of life, our ability to be "at home" and to sustain friendships and a sense of belonging becomes more difficult. In place of genuine community, we design various forms of collectivism. These can be as innocuous as being a "fan" (short for "fanatic") of a sports team or an entertainer. They can be as deadly as being under a totalitarian government, or caught up in a religious cult. None of these can ever fill the void of loneliness implicit in a culture of possessive individualism.

Here I rest my case and conclude this testimony, realizing that what I have written cannot stand as proof, only as an invitation to reflection upon your own experience and be open to the invitation to walk the path toward freedom. I submit to you that the world of possessive individualism, with its distorted sense of faith and freedom, is self-destructive and enslaving. We do not have to live in such a world. We can be free. I offer you what has been offered to me and to all of us, that we are made for a world in which we can trust the promise of freedom, and walk toward it together on the path of covenant relationships, through the gift of forgiving love. Let it be so.

www.ingramcontent.com/pod-product-compliance
Lightning Source LLC
Chambersburg PA
CBHW060418090426
42734CB00011B/2358